# Acting
# Interactive
# Theatre

# Acting Interactive Theatre

## A Handbook

Gary Izzo

HEINEMANN
Portsmouth, NH

**Heinemann**
A division of Reed Elsevier Inc.
361 Hanover Street
Portsmouth, NH 03801-3912

*Offices and agents throughout the world*

**Library of Congress Cataloging-in-Publication Data**
Izzo, Gary.
    Acting interactive theatre : a handbook / Gary Izzo.
      p. cm.
    ISBN 0-435-07038-X
    1. Theater—Production and direction. 2. Improvisation (Acting)
   3. Participatory theater. I. Title.
    PN2053.I98  1998
    792'.028—dc21                     97-36245
                                          CIP

Editor: Lisa A. Barnett
Production: Elizabeth Valway
Cover design: Jenny Jensen Greenleaf
Manufacturing: Louise Richardson

Printed in the United States of America on acid-free paper
02 01 00 99 98  DA  1 2 3 4 5 6 7 8 9

*This book is dedicated to the
Bless the Mark Players,
past, present, and future.*

# Contents

# About the Author

Gary Izzo was one of the first directors to experiment in the interactive genre. As a teacher, he has trained hundreds of actors in interactive and participatory theatre. As a director and producer he began his work in Renaissance festivals in the 1970's, and founded Creative Entertainment, Inc. a company dedicated to the exploration and production of audience inclusive theatre styles. There he produced outdoor interactive festivals, participatory plays, murder mysteries, and interactive convention show concepts. He is a show director/consultant for the Walt Disney World Co., and has been a founding influence in Disney's use of live actors in interactive show venues. He has designed and developed various interactive shows and attractions there, where he introduced interactive theatre as a convention entertainment concept.

For more information about lectures, workshops, and show design/development consulting by Gary Izzo please write: Interactive Artists, P.O. Box 780212, Orlando, FL 32828.

# About This Book

This book is about workshopping, rehearsing, and maintaining an interactive production. It is designed as a resource for the actor, director, or teacher of interactive theatre, and is presented as a supplement to the concepts in the book *The Art of Play: The New Genre of Interactive Theatre,* by Gary Izzo. *Acting Interactive Theatre* takes a step-by-step approach to creating a show, from casting to maintenance rehearsals. It includes 150 workshop exercises to develop ensemble improv skills, interactive characterization, performance elements, and more.

The rehearsal process outlined in this book assumes that the actor has no prior experience in either improvisation or interactive theatre. Therefore, it may be used as either a resource for the expert in creating an interactive production, or as a complete course for the student of the interactive genre. This process is broken into six phases, which present each component in its proper order. The sequence of steps required to build an interactive production are the same as those required in learning interactive performance, less some of the basics. The chart on page xi is a graphical representation of the whole process presented in this book. Generally, these six phases are intended to

## The Rehearsal Process

Based on a six-week rehearsal schedule

| Play Phase | Preparation Phase | Choices Phase | Development Phase | Technique Phase | Performance Phase |
|---|---|---|---|---|---|
| Morning Warm-Up, Body and Vocal | | | | | |
| Noncompetitive Play | | | | | |
| Freeing the Imagination Workshop | | Improv Scene Work | Improv Narrative Skills | Advanced Improv Skills | |
| Period Style Workshop | | | | | |
| Attractions Rehearsals | | | Scenario Rehearsals | | |
| | Intro Character Elements | Develop Character Choices | Advanced Character Devel. | Develop Character Lazzi and Endowments | |
| | Intro Performance Elements | Develop Semblance | Background | | Develop Show Mythology |
| | | | Scene Work in Character | | Develop Relationships |
| | | | | Interactive Technique | Develop Encounters |

cover a normal, full-time, six-week rehearsal period (about one phase per week), but contain ample material to sustain a semester or more of course work. Experienced interactive artists may think of them as covering four full weeks of rehearsal, by condensing the first four phases into two. The truly ambitious might swing a production in three weeks if an experienced ensemble is already in place.

Just as a weight trainer might use an exercise to develop a particular muscle, I use improv exercises to develop a particular mental process, technique, or aspect of character development. I use a precise set of exercises in a specific order in my workshops, to achieve ensemble and free individual creativity.

Throughout this book, improv and character development exercises are written in a standard format. This format breaks an exercise down into four parts: purpose, description, notes, and comments. The purpose section outlines which function is being exercised—the mental muscle, if you will, that the exercise intends on building. The description section outlines how the exercise is to be set up and run. The notes section provides any necessary tips or cautions for the instructor running the exercise. The comments section includes my notes and observations on the usefulness of the exercise, as well as information on when or how the exercise should be used in the rehearsal process.

It is not intended that each and every exercise be done for each section. Often, a greater number of effective exercises than are necessary have been provided to allow for personal preference. It is also assumed that actors and instructors alike will create new exercises to fill a specific need.

Aside from their theatrical relevance, components of this technique, and indeed the technique as a whole, have a way of actualizing the self in a very powerful and positive way. It is my hope that the process outlined in this book will not only be useful to every form of artist, interactive or otherwise, but will also have meaning for the teacher, the therapist, the parent, the healer, and even the behavioral scientist.

# Preface: What Is Interactive Theatre?

*I*nteractive theatre: *theatre in which the audience actively and spontaneously cocreates with the actor the unfolding drama.*

The interactive stage is an environment that encloses both audience, or "guest," and actor alike. Each guest is, initially or as a matter of course, singularly or as a group, endowed with a role to play. The outcome of any scene may change completely depending upon the actions or response of the guest. These actions or responses continually alter the unfolding drama. The guest, as cocreator, is as responsible for the outcome as the actor.

Interactive characters exist without any acknowledgment of themselves as characters in a fiction. The interactive production is not aware of the audience as an audience, because it views it as part of its own reality. Audience members are merely fellow characters within the illusion.

Because of its spontaneous and unpredictable nature, interactive theatre is rooted in the technique of the improviser. However, there is much that is predetermined in interactive theatre. Structures, or performance elements, are designed and polished as in any style of theatre, but are manipulated in the medium of improvisation. Interactive theatre is not designed to be observed, but to be experienced.

The actor first encourages, then teaches the participants to improvise, and gives them the palette of ideas with which to play. Interactive play is always led by the actor, so the general terms and content of the scene are always within the actor's control, and within the general goals of the production. Interactive theatre brings the audience out of their seats and into the illusion of the stage. There they play alongside the actor within a safe and inviolate play space, or *temenos*.

# Part I

# The Rehearsal Process

# Preparation and Casting 1

*I*nteractive theatre a process-oriented form of theatre. In conventional theatre the result of the rehearsal process is a fixed and unchanging set of actions, but in interactive theatre the result *is* the process. It is the process of creative play, finely honed and polished, and ready for the inclusion of the guests. Creating this result is difficult because a process is always in motion. The only way to do it is to maintain *ensemble*. This is a very overused word in the arts, but here I mean it in its original sense, *insimul*, "at the same time, or all parts working or considered as a whole." A group of actors must work in ensemble in order to bring off this process as a polished work of art. Creating ensemble is one of the main underpinnings of this rehearsal process, and it is where we begin.

## Creating Ensemble

There is a right and a wrong way to create ensemble within a group, and it starts at the top. In essence, you get what you pay for. If you want your cast to be playful, trusting, and supportive of each other, you must treat them with the same trust, support, and playfulness. To rely on their professionalism to "do as I say, not as I do" is as big a cop-out as it is a denial of human nature. Impose a typical employer-employee relationship, or even a typical director-actor relationship, and you have lost before you have begun.

Remember you are creating a temenos: a safe and inviolate place to play, a sacred space for the artist. Creativity can be cultured only in this place. The mood of innocence, acceptance, and support is essential to the creative process. In order for the guest to take part in this temenos, it must first exist within the cast. If temenos is to exist within the cast, it must exist within the theatre administration or production company, or at least the part of the company that regularly comes in contact with the cast.

This is a tall order for some companies. The director as well as the producer must work to provide and protect this space for the artist. When they do support a temenos, the most wonderful and unique events occur. When they don't, their only reward is the mundane.

Many executives, and some directors, will see this mood as pandering to the actor, and fear or resent the implications of a "spoiled artist." True, spoil *anyone* and the implications are clear, but the temenos is not a luxury for the artist; it is a necessity. Many can't see the difference. As you might guess, I am often in the position of explaining my philosophy of arts management to producers, executives, and corporate directors who are in the business of "managing people." I attempt to explain it in a pitch I call "the artist bargain."

## THE ARTIST BARGAIN

Whenever an employee is hired by an employer, a bargain is struck. It may be written down or, as often is the case, it is merely understood. That bargain is always this: "The employee shall perform the duties required of the employer in a competent and painstaking manner to the best of his or her ability, and for those services shall receive a paycheck." The amount doesn't matter, the type of service doesn't matter; it's the bargain that matters, and everyone understands it. Agreed?

Now, whenever an *artist* is hired by an employer, a different bargain is struck. It may be written down or, as is often the case, *mis*understood. This bargain is exactly the same as the employee bargain, but instead of receiving a paycheck, the artist receives a paycheck and something else. The artist, whether actor, writer, painter, poet, sculptor, or whatever, is one whose passionate desire for the creation of beauty brought him or her to the decision at some point to put their passion for that act of creation first. They did this knowing they would probably never make much money at it. The artist's employer provides not only the money to live, but the *means to pursue this passion.* Whether they recognize that or not, the artist bargain is always this: "The artist shall perform the duties required of the employer in a competent and painstaking manner to the best of his or her ability, and for those services shall receive a paycheck, and an environment that allows the artist to fulfill his or her creative promise." Why else would most artists make less than other professionals if not that there is another bargaining chip on the table?

The mistake that so many arts managers make is to make the same bargain with the artist as with any other employee. Oh, they're not better than others—even if they'll have you think they are—but they *are* different. When employers deny their responsibility to provide a supportive creative environment essential to the artist's work and fulfillment, whatever that means for that art, they are in breach of this unwritten contract. When you examine the "temperamental artist" in this light, they appear no more temperamental than your average employee who was promised something and didn't get it.

The artist, like any other person, will take what you give and ask for more. It's as easy to spoil an artist as anyone else. But take away what someone has been promised, or perceived that they have been promised, particularly when they have made personal sacrifices to be where they are, and you'll really see them go bonkers—just like, well, a temperamental artist.

In the artist bargain, a safe and supportive creative environment is that promise. It may look like pandering, but a supported artist will make your profits soar. Notwithstanding, there are always times, whether dealing with an artist or not, when the answer must be, "I'm sorry to disappoint you, but you can't have this—deal with it." Keep your bargain, however, and the artist is as easy to manage as anyone else—if you call managing people easy.

## Directing Interactive Theatre

Directing interactive theatre is not like directing conventional theatre. Directors are by nature controlling creatures. They conceive a vision of the production, and bend everything to the will of that vision. They may dictate the most minute details and so control the audience's whole perception, and the actors' every move. This is true of most theatre forms, but not of interactive theatre.

The interactive actor usurps a significant portion of the power, and therefore the responsibility, of both the dramatist and the director. A director new to the interactive genre may have some control issues to work out. It can get very uncomfortable for a director not to have total control over the end result of a production. This *process theatre* is largely unwritten, and subject to the spontaneity of actor and guest alike. It is, perhaps, a fine line, but the interactive director rules and guides, but cannot control. An organic theatre of this type requires an organic approach to direction. To illustrate, let us imagine the production as a tree.

Some stage directors deal only with the minutiae of the production: voice, inflection, gesture, blocking, scenery, etc. These directors build the tree from the leaves and buds first, then to the branches and trunk—from the outer detail to the inner core of the production. At some point they must breathe life into it, or else this construct remains lifeless and "wooden." It is a big job to create each and every individual leaf, and even harder to make it resemble nature. In interactive theatre, the result is not fixed, so this Pygmalion approach can never work. If you work this way as a director, you have a lot of rethinking to do.

Other directors create first from the roots. They concern themselves with essence, theme, and motive. They make the roots resemble nature, then let the actor create. Before long a trunk grows, and gives way to branches and, finally, leaves. This type of director uses the genius of the actor and allows the creative process to have its way, within the close stewardship of his or her own genius. Such a director will prune and tie and shape the tree, until it looks the way he or she wants it to look. If you work this way, interactive theatre will be a frightening, disarming, and fascinating adventure.

The directors of interactive theatre plant a seed. They give it the elements it needs to create itself, encouraging it with water, nutrients, and sunlight. They stand back in delight and watch nature unfold, guiding and protecting it from outside danger or internal aberration. Their only certainty is of what kind of seed they planted, and so of what kind of tree should grow. This style of direction takes great trust, insight, and above all, patience.

In interactive theatre, the word *director* means *one who points toward an aim or goal*. This direc*t*er lets the process run, and uses a herder's wand to keep the players in bounds and headed down the path devised. This is not for the timid or faint of heart. It takes attentiveness, courage, and self-confidence to tangle with chaos. It takes sensitivity and compassion to harness this natural creative power. In this book, the director's role is one of counselor, guide, nurturer, and protector of the temenos.

## *Preparation*

The rehearsal period for a new interactive show or new cast is usually four to six weeks, depending on the scope of the production. Before casting begins, the interactive play or event should be fully designed. The "writing" of the show should include the following:

- *The choice of subject,* and a full examination of your audience's common assumptions about it.
- *Research of the subject* and the historic period depicted. Isolate the visual and actional differences between that period and today that can be displayed or played in the production; items that define the characters of the production; attitudinal differences of the period and cultural suppositions, beliefs, etc.; the everyday aspects of life as they differ from today; and the unique aspects of the subject. Create a bible for the production.
- *The choice of environment* for the production. When the environment is an existing location, it should be explored fully to take advantage of all opportunities it presents in terms of action. In other cases it is designed. If so, it should support the subject and provide ample opportunity for the occupational activities of the characters.
- *Define the themes* to be revealed or explored in the production. What will be the human insights or social commentary evident in the exploration of the subject?
- *Define the characters.* What occupations best reveal the themes of the production, and provide the most playable and entertaining action within the environment?
- *Choose the event* of the production, or write the overriding scenario. In the interactive event, the *event* is the common activity that every character in the environment can relate to, the reason they are all there—usually some sort of

celebration or ritual. For interactive plays, there may also be a recognizable event, but the key plot points of the story, the elements of action that cannot be changed, must be defined.

- *Research style.* Prepare workshops on the dialect, use of language, movement, customs and manners, dress, and accessories of the period.
- *Prepare scripts for any attractions*, or conventional shows within the interactive show, such as dances or songs.

## Casting

With these elements defined, you will know what you need in an actor in terms of the requirements of the role. There are other things to be considered, however, in choosing an actor for work in interactive theatre.

### BACKGROUND EXPERIENCE

Actors with experience in the same period style may seem important, but it is of far less concern than other experience. Whether they have learned the dialect or know the period is less important than whether they are any good at learning them. Assume that you will teach the styles you need in rehearsals since you will have to give the company a common base in any case. Don't be lulled into thinking that since they can handle the style, they can handle the interactive work. If they can handle period styles at all, you can teach it in rehearsals.

Experience in improvisation is more important. Almost any type of experience in improv is useful, whether or not it was good training. You can quickly determine their skill level in auditions, and decide if they can be trained in the rehearsal time you have.

Interactive experience is best. I always ask actors what kind of performance experience they have had where they speak directly to, or interact with, the audience. Most often the answer is children's theatre, in which they had to get the audience to respond or bring kids up on stage to do something. Any experience that required them to deal directly with the audience at least lets you know they are not afraid of audience intimacy.

### ENSEMBLE SKILLS

Every audition for interactive theatre must include an improv callback. There is simply no way to determine if they are right for spontaneous theatre other than to see them do it. I usually run a freeze tag scene so that I can rotate a number of actors through at once. It's quicker, and you usually don't need much in order to see what you need to see.

In preparing for the exercise, I create as casual an atmosphere as I can. To those who may dread improvising for an audition, I say to look at the bright side: they can't possibly prepare for it, so they might as well relax and have fun. I also tell them that although what we do is comic, I am not looking for how hysterically funny they are in these scenes, but how well they work with their partner, how well they share the scene and build it together. This takes off the pressure to come up with a big punch line, and lets them know what I am really concerned with.

Indeed, good ensemble skills are the hallmark of good interactive theatre. Those who play for the laugh only, or for control, or for gain at their partner's expense will not only be limiting in an interactive ensemble, but detrimental. If there is anything I consider a solid head start from casting, it is actors with good listening skills, and a willingness to support and let their partner play.

### OUTWARD ENERGY AND PLAYFULNESS

Perhaps the most important aspect of casting for an interactive show is the least tangible. It is more a quality of personality than of skill. Some people just seem more playful. They have an outward energy that invites you in; they twinkle. These playful people take delight in others. You get the feeling that they are interested in others not because of what they stand to gain, but merely because they are interested, and that their interest alone has value enough for them. They never seem fearful, or judgmental, particularly of themselves. Above all, they give you the impression that, bottom line, beneath the inevitable everyday doubts, they *approve of themselves*. A person in touch with his or her sense of innocence and joy will always make a good interactive performer.

### USING "VETERANS"

Any actor who has done interactive performance before is likely to feel they have nothing new to learn in rehearsal. Even if they are veterans I trained myself, I make a point of putting them through the same rehearsal process as everyone else. There is always something new to learn, and their experience will help the process. Most important, developing temenos in an ensemble does not start with a class system. I ask my experienced actors for their support and assistance in the process, which must be newly created with each cast.

Experienced improvisers often feel that basic exercises are somehow beneath them. You may find a lack of commitment from them in early rehearsals. This betrays an attitude that needs illuminating. I believe that often what they are "saying" with this behavior is, "I need you to know that I know this." Indeed they do, and it is important that you as director let them know you recognize and value their hard-earned experience. But discipline and practice are part of every art; the concert pianist still practices his scales, the prima ballerina still does her barre, the painter still fills stacks of sketchbooks. Although they are proficient at these exercises, committing to them still improves their skill. The improviser as artist is not exempt from this. A good director will make this clear, and impose a little discipline.

## Orientation

First impressions are lasting, and when creating an ensemble they are crucial to your success. I believe that the very first moments a new cast is together are the most formative in terms of creating a supportive ensemble. For this "imprinting" process, I like to have the first gathering of the group be an informal reception, or party. All actors, production, and management people attend. Here as people mingle and meet each other, the professional status lines are blurred. The casual setting lets the cast know that everyone is human and potentially friendly. It gives a sense of community and commonality, and allows the bonds of trust to begin.

The first rehearsal day is set aside for orientation. It should start with resolving logistical concerns, to reduce fears and create a feeling of security. Issues like money, paydays, housing, transportation, and schedules should be presented in a well-ordered and efficient way. Resolving these concerns right at the start will go a long way toward reducing fears and anticipation of what is to come, and give the impression that they are in safe and organized hands. Areas like roles, what workshops cover, how rehearsals will be conducted, and how the performance will flow should be discussed. If they can form a picture in their minds of what they are embarking upon, they can let it go when the work begins, and be more present.

It is a good idea to convey the artistic goals of the production. I don't mean how many people will show up or how much they'll enjoy it, but what you want them to walk away with. How do you want them to feel and what insights do you hope they will emerge with at the end of the show? This is that path the interactive director guides them along. A clear view of this at the outset will not only make directing easier, but may also instill in the cast a sense of purpose that will bring the group together.

A tour of the performance space is helpful here if it can be arranged. Again, it gives them a frame of reference for the work, and can also fire the imagination. I like to conduct a walk-through with the whole group, acting as a sort of tour guide. I explain each area's practical function, stopping to point out specific locations where important actions or scenarios unfold. I try to give a blow-by-blow account of the show or performance day, and paint as colorful a picture as I can of how the production flows.

Actors should have the earliest possible notion of how their character will look, and how much latitude they will have in creating it. Some show designs impose more givens on characterization. The costume design must often be set before the character is through the development process. The actors must know at the start what aspects of the character cannot change, and how far they are allowed to accessorize the look. The director must define the boundaries of their creative "sandbox," if you will, to let them know where and how far they can play.

Another early endeavor of mine is to make personal contact with each individual in the ensemble, and try to maintain a consistency with it thereafter. Paradoxically, creating a group identity also requires an individual identity. Each actor must be made to feel that they have their own unique place within the ensemble, that they offer something that no one else can, and that that is why they are there. It is another fact of nature that group consciousness doesn't work without a strong individual consciousness. I find that much of my work as director lies in creating and maintaining these identities.

Warm-ups may be taught during orientation. I insist on doing a complete body warm-up as a group, at the start of every rehearsal day. The twenty-minute warm-up consists mostly of stretching and isolations, but covers every muscle group. I have found it to be an incredible tool: it energizes the cast for rehearsals, builds breath and stamina, helps with vocal production and physicalization, and reduces injury. I first began these warm-ups at the Sterling Renaissance Festival, where the day-long event spanned a rugged wooded terrain. Falls, cuts, bruises, and sprains plagued us. After the institution of the warm-up, they virtually stopped!

Now, let's face it: few of us like the idea of a formal morning warm-up. It sounds like boot camp. True, I get some grumbles and groans at first. But, amazingly, after the first week or so they will grumble if you cancel it. They always come to prefer the warm-up, once it becomes routine and they feel its results. A powerful side effect is that it focuses the group. The act of a common ritual each day galvanizes the group's sense of community. By the way, I have a rule that anyone present at the warm-up *must* take part in it, no exceptions—including me.

Finally, I conclude the orientation process with building familiarity within the group. The more the cast knows about each other, the easier it is for them to extend their trust. Do enough group introductions and you will soon see that we westerners define ourselves more by what we *do* than who we *are*.

Ask an actor for instance, to give some background on him- or herself and you will more than likely hear about their training and experience in the theatre, including that touring company gig with so-and-so. Of course there is nothing wrong with this in itself, but the message is, "I am only so good as what I have done." Let that discussion continue, and as each person speaks, status lines are drawn based on who has the most or best experience. When it's over, you have a group more divided and insecure than before.

One of the most important underpinnings of interactive theatre is its affirmation of the guests as special just as they are, for *who* they are, without the need for justification. This then is the first obstacle to tackle within the ensemble. I have a lovely exercise, given to me by a valued colleague, that very neatly deletes the "ego" from the "intro."

## Biographies

---

PURPOSE: To share background without the burden of self-consciousness. To experience the supportive feeling of hearing others talk about you in a positive way.

DESCRIPTION: The group pairs off. Player One has three to five minutes to interview Player Two about who they are, and take notes. Explain that this is a "Barbara Walters" interview, in-depth, but fair and respectful. P1 may ask about P2's professional experience, goals, personal life, friendships, family life, childhood background, special moments, etc. P2 may be given a moment at the end, to add anything else he or she feels appropriate. Players switch, P2 interviews P1. When this is done, each player is given one minute to reveal to the whole group *who* their partner is. Their partner may coach them if they forget details, but *only if asked*.

NOTES:   1. Before beginning, coach players on the types of questions they may ask in order to understand who their partner is.
   2. Remind players to speak *positively and respectfully* about their partner. They are never to be flippant or sarcastic, or to make commentary on what they have heard, but only to relay the information in the spirit in which it was given.

COMMENTS: This exercise can take some time if it is a large group, but it is worthwhile because it will save a lot of posturing and uncertainty during the rehearsal process.

## *Starting Rehearsals*

At the beginning and end of each rehearsal day, I perform a ritual exercise that calls upon the actor to be deliberate in checking in and checking out of the temenos. It begins with the group standing in a circle and holding hands. I ask them to close their eyes, breathe deep, and relax. I use this moment to make affirmative remarks or set challenges for the rehearsal day. I may ask them to release their tensions, fears, and judgments, to visualize the day's goals realized, to offer their trust, to agree to play, or to address any other aspect of the work that needs focus or encouragement. I ask them to open a circle of play, and to allow a temenos to be created for the day's rehearsal. I then segue into the "Harmony" exercise, which follows, and then on to the physical warm-up. We rejoin this circle at the end of the day, and as the sound fades from the Harmony exercise, so does the temenos.

   The ritual of it often makes the actors a little self-conscious to begin with, but afterward you will never get away with starting a rehearsal without it. Although we are unfamiliar with ritual, we also crave it—often desperately. Its psychological importance is to mentally mark the beginning and ending of creative play, to let our subconscious know when these alternate rules of thought apply. It also affords them time to focus their attention on the ensemble, and tune in to its collective energy.

## Harmony

PURPOSE: To harmonize group energy.

DESCRIPTION: The entire group stands in a tight circle facing inward, and holds hands. They close their eyes and breathe a few deep breaths, in through the nose and out the mouth. (Here the instructor may ask them to assess their personal state of being, and make affirmations about setting everyday concerns aside.) They are then to hear (only in their mind) a single tone that seems to them to be their current frequency or vibration. The *sound* of their mood. On the instructor's cue, they hum that pitch in a continuous "maa" sound. The resulting harmony or dissonance can be seen as a measure of ensemble harmony. The instructor then coaches them to move the sound to a harmonic chord; they slowly step forward until bunched together, and play with the sound until asked for it to slowly fade to silence. The circle then opens, and play space is declared.

NOTES: The instructor should warn players not to verbalize their personal tone until asked, because hearing it may affect the tone of others in the group.

COMMENTS: This exercise is a good precursor to the HRC warm-up. I have also used it as an indicator to myself, or as proof to the group, that they are not working together in a harmonic fashion. It may seem strange, but the level of harmonics in the unbidden chord does relate to the group's level of cooperation and mutual sensitivity.

I employ another type of "warm-up" before improv or character workshops, or after a long break, to encourage closeness and soften personal barriers. I believe it is crucial that breaking down personal barriers between performers be a gentle, even enjoyable experience. I have never seen any value in brutal and traumatic "break-through sessions," other than making the instructor feel powerful.

## HRC Warm-Up (Hugs, Rubs, and Compliments)

PURPOSE: To create a positive, relaxing, and intimate mood for rehearsal.

DESCRIPTION: The group forms a single-file line, one behind the other. Each player gives a shoulder rub to the player in front. After a few moments, players are asked to turn around, and rub the person behind them. When that is complete, each player is asked to mill about the room exchanging hugs with each other player they randomly encounter, trying before the allotted time is up to hug each and every player. During (or after) the hug session, the instructor asks players to exchange compliments. Compliments may be deep or shallow, but *always* positive (never backhanded). In each encounter, the complimented player never "returns the compliment" but responds with a simple "thank you," and moves on. This is done so that actors learn to accept what is good about them, without feeling as though they need to immediately give it back. When players have gotten to most other players in the group, the warm-up is concluded.

NOTES:  1. Variations on the shoulder rub may be performed, such as the rubbing of arms, hands, head, or even feet.
2. In exchanging hugs, players may simply say "good morning" or the person's name, but are not to engage in conversation.
3. Players are not to judge the quality of their compliments; it may be as simple as, "I like your necklace," or as deep as, "I appreciate your generosity."
4. For each encounter, whoever speaks first is the initiator of the compliment. (The instructor may later choose to allow an exchange of compliments, or qualify what type of compliment can be given, such as a general compliment, or a compliment on their work or behavior.)

COMMENTS: This is a marvelous all-purpose "emotional warm-up." It is a great emotional conditioner and relaxer to prepare groups for ensemble work. By the way, the instructor should always be a participant. If you are too good to accept a hug, or pay a compliment to your cast yourself, you will never lead them to a true ensemble.

# *Play Phase* 2

*T*his first phase of rehearsals connects the actor with the experience of play, and begins the process of freeing the imagination. It includes beginning any necessary workshops in period style, and may involve rehearsals of scripted material for attractions.

## Noncompetitive Play

The actor must first get in touch with the feeling of play. We begin this phase with simple childhood games, and play until the bonds of play form. Emphasize nonjudgment, and make fun the only goal. Play any kind of game except games of competition. There should never be a "winner" and a "loser." You may not have grown up with many noncompetitive games yourself, but many cultures are full of childhood games where there need be no victor or vanquished. Native American culture has loads of them. Many are so simple they may not even seem like games to you. Play with blocks, make mud pies, fingerpaint, play make-believe. Play tag, or hide-and-seek; these can be played without a winner/loser. The company may remember noncompetitive games from their childhood; if so, try them. If you hear the comment, "We get paid for this?" you're on the right track.

The director should motivate their play so as to give them experiences in all the aspects of play. (See Chapter One of *The Art of Play*.) You can later connect to those experiences in rehearsal. They need to experience play directly, not through lecture or discussion. Don't talk about the process; just do it. Give them a visceral connection to how play feels. When asked about the process—which you will be at this early stage, when all they are doing is playing hide-and-seek—give short, honest answers. Ask for their trust, and assure them that everything they are being asked to do has a purpose.

## Hide-and-Seek

PURPOSE: To experience noncompetitive play.

DESCRIPTION: Players use the performance environment as a playground for hide-and-seek. The seeker closes his or her eyes and counts to twenty while all other players find a hiding spot, then begins the search. Each hider that is found becomes a seeker. Hiders may change their hiding place, but as soon as they are seen, they become seekers.

COMMENTS: There are many variations to this favorite childhood game. Feel free to try any you know, or have the company make up a new version.

## Tag Games

PURPOSE: To experience noncompetitive physical play.

DESCRIPTION: Game boundaries for the playing area are set and one player is chosen as "it." "It's" objective is to touch or "tag" other players. Here are some of the many variations to this game. *Freeze tag:* Each tagged player is frozen in place until the end of the game, or until another free player unfreezes them by touching them. *Safety tag* is played using one or more players as "safeties." Any free player in physical contact with a safety may not be tagged or frozen. In *hug tag* a player can only be safe if hugging a specified number of other players. The instructor calls out the number of huggers required to be safe, and changes the number at will. *Compliment tag* proceeds just as freeze tag, except that to be unfrozen, one player must touch the frozen player and offer a genuine personal compliment. *Blob tag:* When "it" catches someone they join hands. Now they are the blob. As each new person is caught, they become part of the blob. As the blob grows, it may split itself apart and organize its attacks. Boundaries are set for this version so that players can be cornered.

NOTES: Tag games with a large group may have more than one "it." In some versions, the instructor may call out new "its" during the game, or switch "its" and "safeties."

COMMENTS: Tag games are good play because they are energetic and involve physical contact. Some may also be used for the Trust section that follows.

## Go Tag

PURPOSE: To experience noncompetitive physical play.

DESCRIPTION: This is a version of tag played with great strategy in India. Everyone squats in a line, alternate players facing opposite directions. The player at one end is the first runner; the player at the other end is the first chaser. The chase happens in an oval track around the line of squatters, as in a steeplechase. The runner may run in either direction, clockwise or counterclockwise, but the chaser may run in only one direction (of their own choosing). As the chaser passes any of the squatters in the line, he/she may tap one on the back and shout "Go!" The tagged player jumps up and continues the chase (still in only one direction), while the old chaser takes the squatter's place in the line. In this way, chasers can change direction or cutoff the runner. When the runner is tagged, he/she squats at the end of the line. the chaser is now the runner, and the player at the other end of the line becomes the new chaser.

NOTES: There is a great deal of strategy to this game. The simplest is to tap a new chaser, facing the appropriate direction, to cutoff the runner just as he/she rounds the turn at the end of the line.

COMMENTS: This very energetic game calls for great cooperation and team play.

## People Knots

PURPOSE: To experience noncompetitive physical play.

DESCRIPTION: Eight to twelve players stand shoulder to shoulder in a circle, and place their hands into the center. To tie the knot, each player now grabs a couple of hands (one hand for each of theirs). No one can hold both hands of the same person, or the hand of a person directly to either side of them. Climbing through and around each other, the group endeavors to untangle the knot. Players may pivot their grips, but may not break their hold. When the knot is untied, they will be left with a ring of players holding hands, or in some cases two interconnected rings of players.

COMMENTS: This one is always a favorite. It uses cooperation and supportive physical contact.

## Dragon's Horde

PURPOSE: To experience noncompetitive physical play.

DESCRIPTION: Player One is chosen as the dragon to stand guard over his jewels. A handkerchief acts as the jewels. Other players circle around the dragon and try to steal his jewels without being tagged. The jewel-catcher must get completely away from the dragon's grasp to succeed. Tagged players are frozen until the end of the game. The game ends when all are frozen (very rare) or when someone steals the jewels. The jewel-catcher plays the next dragon.

NOTES:  1. The dragon may range as far from the jewels as he/she dares, but it's a good idea to get right on top of them. Dragons do not last long in this game.
2. Some common strategies include: reaching between the dragon's legs, making believe you are frozen, or an all-out group charge.

COMMENTS: This one is fast and furious! Ask players to be fair and honest about whether they have been tagged.

## Red Handed

PURPOSE: To experience noncompetitive physical play.

DESCRIPTION: Eight to twelve players form a circle and one chosen as "it" stands in the center. "It" closes his/her eyes as a small object such as a marble is passed, unseen, from hand to hand. "It" signals and opens his/her eyes. Who has the marble? If "it" detects a suspicious face he/she taps one of the players' fists. If the hand is empty, "it" moves on. Meanwhile, the marble continues to be passed behind "it's" back. Fake passes, decoys, and innocent looks are an important part of this game. When "it" catches someone red handed, he/she joins the circle and the caught player is the new "it."

COMMENTS: This game engenders eye contact and playful foolery.

## Yogi Tag

PURPOSE: To experience noncompetitive physical play.

DESCRIPTION: The playing area is divided into two equal parts with a clear center line; tape or string works well. The playing area should be a soft surface. Two teams stand on either side of the center line, leaving playing space between them. Team One chooses a player to make a dash across the center line and tag as many players from Team Two as possible, and return safely to the home side. Before crossing the center line, the player must take one deep breath and use it to repeat in a loud and steady, rapid flow, the sound, "Dho-dho-dho-dho-dho. . . ." If members of the opposite team (Team Two) catch and hold the player (or Dho-dho") until he/she runs out of breath, the Dho-dho joins their team. If the Dho-dho makes it back across the center line, all the players he/she tagged become part of the Dho-dho's team. The Dho-dho can only be touched above the waist, and must be gently held until they can no longer say, "Dho." Teams alternate sending Dho-dhos across the center line to tag players. The game is over when all players are on one team.

COMMENTS: One variation is that tagged players are out of the game, so long as the Dho-dho made it back across the center line. Play proceeds until one team is out of players.

## Freeing the Imagination

*Imagining should be as effortless as perceiving.*
As actors become reacquainted with childhood play, use the Freeing the Imagination workshop to help them awaken their creative self and empower their spontaneity. These two rehearsal components complement each other, and are an important precursor to workshops in improvisation technique. So many teachers of improv start with the technique, or "rules of improv," and go from there. These rules assume the players have confidence in their creativity, and the capacity for spontaneity, but do little to develop them. If the art of improvisation is the manipulation of spontaneous thought into a coherent form, how then does one learn to be spontaneous? We use this minicourse in creativity to kick-start the improv process and encourage good ensemble skills.

This material deals directly with the actors' relationship to their own creative imagination, allowing them to come to terms with their own creative power *before* applying it to a group. The areas of Trust, Spontaneity, Free Association, and Incorporation are explored in the following sections. If the time and care is taken now to release individual fears and self-judgment, it will place the actor light-years ahead in improv technique and character development.

The first half of this course in creative thinking takes place in this phase, the second half in the next. (See Chapter Eleven in *The Art of Play.*)

TRUST

*Trust is given, not earned, and it always represents risk.*
The exercises that follow provide methods for building trust in a group by building familiarity and dispelling fears. The problem of building self-trust (or trust in one's own creative power) begins here, but is continued in the Spontaneity section. These exercises should feel to the cast like an extension of the childhood games listed previously, and should be approached in the same playful spirit. Again, they don't need to understand their purpose so much as to feel their effect.

Do them early in the rehearsal day. Continue one or two per day at least through the play phase and perhaps into the next. Let the ensemble's comfort level and willingness to rely on each other be your gauge.

## Falling

PURPOSE: To teach the body to trust, and to break down physical barriers in the group.

DESCRIPTION: Six to eight players stand in a tight circle facing inward, shoulder to shoulder, no gaps. Player One stands in the center with feet and legs tight together, and arms folded across chest. Standing relaxed but rigid, with eyes closed, P1 leans backward until supported by the outer players. Outer players gently toss P1 around in a circle pivoting him or her by the feet. Tossing should be gentle and shallow at first, then gradually increased as P1 becomes more comfortable. After a minute or two the outer players stand P1 upright; P1 opens his/her eyes. Each outer player then takes a turn in the center.

NOTES: 1. Counsel outer players to brace themselves by placing one foot behind them. Outer players must support P1 with their whole bodies, not just their arms.
2. Explain to all that P1 is placing his or her personal safety in their hands. Trust is a responsibility that must be taken seriously.
3. As the exercise goes on, outer players will tend to take more chances, and will tire. Caution outer players that each new P1 is "falling" for the first time; remind them to be sensitive to the player in the middle.

COMMENTS: This exercise is very useful for a new ensemble and tends to "break the ice" physically and allow the group to have a little fun together while building important trust. It should be used early in rehearsals.

## Falling—Variation

PURPOSE: To develop trust within a group through teaching the body to trust (advanced).

DESCRIPTION: Eight to ten players kneel around Center Player, who lies on floor, face up, arms to sides, legs together, eyes closed. Each Outer Player places their hands in a supporting position beneath Center Player's shoulders, torso, hips, thighs, calves, and head. On cue, Outer Players lift Center Player to waist height. Center Player remains relaxed but rigid. On cue,

Center Player is lifted in one smooth motion from waist height to over their heads, arms extended, and walked around the room. Outer Players then lower Center Player to waist height, then, on cue, gently but swiftly toss Center Player straight into the air where he will be suspended for an instant unsupported, then caught, and returned to waist height. Center Player is set on his feet, and a new Center Player is chosen.

NOTES:  1. Be sure that each Outer Player understands that they are entrusted with responsibility for the Center Player's safety.
2. Coach Outer Players that they are working as one, and concentrate on lifting and tossing Center Player in a smooth and continuously balanced motion.

COMMENTS: This exercise accomplishes the same objectives as the falling exercise, except it is a little scarier, and is best used after the falling exercise. It is a physically tiring exercise, so care must be taken that the group is not too tired by the time the last person is lifted. I also recommend that the heaviest person be lifted first, saving the lightest for last.

## First Good Impressions

PURPOSE: To learn the positive aspects of one's self-image as perceived by others. To build self-confidence and self-esteem.

DESCRIPTION: The group stands facing each other in two equal lines. Each player finds their partner in the opposite line and stands directly in front of them. Partners take turns telling the other the first good impression they had of them dating from whenever they first met (about one minute each). All pairs perform this task simultaneously. When the pair to the right of each player is finished, that player steps to the right to stand directly in front of their new partner. They exchange first good impressions. This process continues until each player has spoken with every other player in the group. When a player reaches the end of the line, he or she joins the end of the other line. The two lines will roll like the tread of a tank, until finally the original pairs are reached and everyone has been spoken to. (Trust me, it works!)

NOTES:  1. Require all players to agree to forgive their partner in advance for struggling to recall a good impression.

Understand that it is often difficult to recall and verbalize these impressions.

2. Impressions need not necessarily be deep, but must
be honest. "I noticed your beautiful hair" is as
acceptable as "You exuded a warmth and kindness
of spirit that made me feel comfortable and welcome."

3. Impressions must never be backhanded, e.g.: "I realized you were much nicer than people had told me."
They must be completely positive perceptions.

4. Coach the group gently but continuously to move the
exercise along, and to take only so much time as
they need to explain their good impressions.

COMMENTS: This is a very powerful exercise. For some it will
be their very first positive feedback on how others perceive
them. We mostly receive criticism in terms of what can be
improved. We rarely get feedback on what is already good about
us. Run this exercise after group members have had a chance to
form impressions of one another, but still early on in the
rehearsal process. This exercise can take a while, but will create
an immense amount of positive energy within the ensemble. As
the exercise goes on, each player will discover patterns to piece
together a picture of how they are positively perceived by other
people. At the end of this exercise, the group will be walking six
feet above the ground!

## Mirror

PURPOSE: To learn to tune in to another player, and follow or
initiate smoothly and seamlessly.

DESCRIPTION: The group pairs up. All pairs perform simultaneously. Players One and Two stand before each other, each treat-
ing the other as their full-length mirror image. P1 first initiates
movements, while P2 follows. When the instructor calls
"Switch!" P2 initiates and P1 follows. Instructor continues to call
"Switch!" for several cycles, until finally ending with the word
"Both!" at which point *both* players attempt to follow the other—
seamlessly.

NOTES: Players should begin their movements small and slow,
and then challenge each other by increasing their complexity

and speed. Facial expressions should also be mirrored. The initiator's objective is not to stump, but to challenge their partner, and lead them to a heightened state of sensitivity.

COMMENTS: This old stand-by still works so well. I also use a more complex version that involves one player as initiator and three as followers, as though a single person were standing in front of a three-sided mirror, such as one would find in a clothing store. The different angles involved can get fairly tricky.

## Mirror Conversation

PURPOSE: To learn to tune in to a partner on a vocal level.

DESCRIPTION: The group pairs up, and each pair performs the exercise simultaneously. A topic of conversation is chosen and Player One begins speaking extemporaneously on that topic without pause. Player Two mirrors Player One by repeating his or her words and inflections, striving to make it sound as though both are speaking simultaneously. When the instructor calls "Switch!" P2 then begins initiating speech, picking up seamlessly where P1 left off. P1 immediately begins mirroring P2's speech. The instructor calls "Switch!" for four or five cycles making the time between switches shorter and shorter, and finally calls "Both!" whereupon *both* players attempt to mirror each other's speech without initiating.

NOTES   1. The initiator's objective is not to stump the partner, but to speak fast enough to continually keep him or her challenged—to lead the partner to a more acute sensitivity to the initiator's speech.
2. When the instructor calls "Switch!" the roles of initiator and mirrorer change seamlessly and without pause. When the instructor calls "Both!" neither player should consciously initiate new dialogue, instead, both attempt to continue to follow.

COMMENTS: This is also a good listening exercise, since so much concentration must be focused on what the other person is saying. To make it more complex you might try adding physical mirroring to the verbal mirroring. Then, if you really want to be cruel, you can add the layer of one person initiating the speech, while the other person initiates the movement.

# Echo

PURPOSE: To experience "tuning outward" and reacting as part of a whole.

DESCRIPTION: Six to twelve players lie in a circle, shoulder to shoulder, with the top of their heads pointing to the center of the circle. Players hold hands. Player One is chosen to send a movement clockwise around the circle by squeezing the hand of the person to their right. Players move the squeeze around the circle as fast as possible. Later, a counterclockwise squeeze is added by Player Two at the opposite side of the circle, and words are attached to each squeeze; "zip" for clockwise squeezes; "zap" for counterclockwise squeezes. When players are proficient they move on to Part 2.

Part 2: "Zip" and "zap" are replaced by words of a sentence called out by P1, one word at a time, as if shouting it into a canyon to hear the echo (e.g., "I . . . have . . . a . . . big . . . echo"). Players echo each word clockwise around the circle. Like a real echo, each word is softer than the previous. P1 waits for the softest echo to reach him before shouting the next word. Later, the exercise is restarted and a P2, across the circle from P1, simultaneously shouts out a different sentence that is echoed in a counterclockwise motion.

NOTES: Players are to focus their awareness on the whole circle, not merely their part of it. They should *feel* the squeeze or sound as it travels around the circle. Remind them that they are connected to everyone in the circle at all times.

COMMENTS: This is a good exercise for focusing the group's awareness on the idea of unity and wholeness. It should be conducted in a focused but playful manner.

## Blind Barn Animals

PURPOSE: To tune in to each other on an audio level, and to provide playful physical contact.

DESCRIPTION: Group members, less a few spotters, are asked to stand in the center of a room cleared of obstacles and raise one hand into the air. The instructor steps through the crowd counting them off into groups of four, pulling each player's arms down as they are counted. This is done quickly so that players are not aware of who else in the group has their number. With eyes closed, the players are asked to *mill and seethe* (or shuffle themselves about). For each number, the instructor calls out the name of a barnyard animal, such as a sheep, a goat, a pig, a cow, a dog, or a chicken. Players are then asked to find their like animals using only the animal's call to locate their kin. Spotters aid in redirecting strays back into the group. When one player finds another like animal, they are to attach themselves and continue looking for additional brethren. The exercise is over when all animals have found their full groups.

NOTES: Caution players to take care in a blind mill and seethe exercise not to make any fast movements or thrust arms or legs out abruptly.

COMMENTS: This is a good warm-up exercise for an improv session because it is physical and fun. It can get quite loud, too.

## Blind Leading the Blind

PURPOSE: To teach group trust without eyesight.

DESCRIPTION: The entire group forms a single-file line, one behind the other. Each player places his or her hands on the hips or shoulders of the player in front as in a conga line. The lead player keeps his or her eyes open, while all others behind him keep their eyes closed. The lead player leads the group in a snakelike motion throughout the room or environment.

NOTES:  1. Players should keep their eyes closed at all times. They are safe from obstacles as long as they remain behind the person in front of them.
2. The lead player is instructed to lead the group around in increasingly complex patterns as the exercise goes on.
3. Several spotters should be named to aid in repairing a broken line or a line that slides too close to an obstacle.

COMMENTS: This exercise gives you an eerie feeling of being under your own power, yet at the same time being completely dependent on being led.

## Find Your Friend Blind

PURPOSE: To develop trust and physical awareness, by breaking the intimacy barrier.

DESCRIPTION: The group pairs up. Partners take a few moments to explore how they would distinguish their partner from the rest of the group using only their hands. They explore the textures of their partner's hair, clothing, facial features, etc. They explore the placement of jewelry, style of clothing, their partner's height, and so on. Players then congregate in the center of the room, close their eyes, and place their hands in front of their chests, close to their bodies, palms outward. Taking *small careful steps* they mill and seethe about the space, until they have completely lost their partner. Spotters should be chosen to guard the perimeter to protect players from straying into furniture or walls. Without making telltale sounds of any kind, players are to find their partner, by touch only. When players believe they have found their partner, they latch on and move carefully toward the perimeter of the space. They open their eyes; if their partner is indeed their own, they withdraw from the space and assist the other spotters. If they are wrong, they close their eyes immediately, and reenter the space to resume their search. The exercise is over when all partners are reunited. A second part to this exercise proceeds as the first, except players may not use their hands to make contact with their partners. Hands must remain folded in front or behind the player at all times. Players are to explore the textures, etc., of their partner using any part of their body, e.g., head, mouth, and shoulders. Players may also use their sense of smell to distinguish players.

NOTES: Remind players to *move slowly* and *take tiny steps* so that collisions with other players are soft, not painful. Likewise, they should hold their hands protectively in front of them, but close to their bodies, and avoid any sharp movements.

COMMENTS: This exercise is a gentle and enjoyable way of breaking physical barriers between ensemble members.

## Hug a Tree

PURPOSE: To develop outward awareness and find connection with a natural environment.

DESCRIPTION: In an outdoor rehearsal or performance environment, each player is sent out to find their favorite tree. To do this, they walk alone, focusing their awareness outward, and search for a tree that seems to call to them. They may think of it as letting the *tree* find *them*. Once they identify a tree they are particularly drawn to, they are to sit quietly for a few moments, focusing their attention only on the tree. They may lean against it, wrap their arms and/or legs around it, climb it, etc. After they have been still a few moments, focusing on the life force of the tree, they may then speak to it and ask it questions (they may do this out loud or in their minds). They should give themselves time to perceive the tree's reply, and give themselves over entirely to their imagination and the living presence of the tree.

NOTES:  1. Players may experience feelings, emotions, and/or messages from their trees.
2. Remind players to feel, in empathy, the entire presence of the tree, from branch tips through to its deepest roots. Try to feel its connection to the earth and sky.

COMMENTS: Players will often be surprised, even overwhelmed, by the responses they receive from their tree. They will often bond with that tree in a way they will not forget. (It is fascinating how different people at different times will perceive the same "personality" of a particular tree.) From an acting perspective, this exercise gives actors a visceral connection to, and a deeper respect for, the natural environment. This is particularly important for shows where the performance environment is outdoors. Any person of a preindustrial era had a deeper connection to the earth and its cycles than we do. Any reconnection made will greatly enhance a character's believability within a natural performance environment.

## Tread Roll

PURPOSE: To release physical inhibitions in the ensemble.

DESCRIPTION: No more than a dozen players lie on their backs on the floor. Players should lie very tightly together (this is important), shoulder to shoulder, hip to hip, with their arms over their heads. The player on one end rolls over on top of the player next to him or her, keeping raised arms, and continues to roll along the line of players to the end of the line. The next player follows immediately after the first, rolling over on top of the other players in the line, creating a sort of tank tread effect. The exercise is over when all players have rolled through the line once. Several spotters may be required to help players who become misaligned or get stuck.

NOTES: The instructor should caution actors to be polite. (Women should be cautioned as to where their knees are placed!)

COMMENTS: Attempt this exercise only after the ensemble is comfortable with each other physically. It is pretty much the end of the line for physical inhibition exercises.

## Contact Improv Dance

PURPOSE: To explore physical spontaneity between ensemble members.

DESCRIPTION: The instructor puts on music for the group to dance to. (Music of a sweeping dramatic style works well.) Players are to perform an interpretive dance to the music, while *at all times* remaining in physical contact with at least one other player. Players may move from one player to the next, but physical contact must never be broken. You may start this exercise with partners first, then allow group movement.

NOTES: Coach players not to merely dance for themselves, but to create a dance *with* their partner (or partners). Coach players to *Make eye contact! Feel the music! Let your movements flow! Share your movement! Connect and explore your movement with others! Make contact with every part of your body, not just your arms and hands!*

COMMENTS: The Mirror exercise is an excellent warm-up for Contact Improv Dance. I will often run the two together. I think this exercise should be performed in the spirit of fun. At its essence, this exercise explores sharing movement with another. Their focus should be on the bodies of their partner(s), not on themselves.

## The Eye Game

PURPOSE: To increase the player's perceptual awareness.

DESCRIPTION: Players pair up. Pairs may play this game simultaneously. Partners stand or sit directly in front of each other. Player One closes his or her eyes. Player Two chooses one of their partner's closed eyes to focus upon, and stares with both eyes directly and intensely at the one eye. P1 tries to *feel* which eye is being stared at. When the P1s feel they know, they open the eye they believe is being stared at. If their partner is staring back, they are correct, if they are staring at the other eye, they are incorrect. Players switch roles and repeat.

NOTES:  1. Players should not merely look at the eyelid, but focus their awareness on being seen by the eye behind the lid.
2. Receiving players must relax and feel, not think. Let their other perceptions tell them which eye is being focused upon. Let their imaginations, not their reason, rule.

COMMENTS: This exercise is not so impossible as it may seem. (My own success rate is better than 90 percent.) When players can feel the proof of perception beyond their reasoning faculties, they can begin to rely upon and trust the intuitive processes.

## Moving Through Obstacles

PURPOSE: To develop an intuitive awareness between performance partners.

DESCRIPTION: An obstacle course is set up using chairs or other players, for instance, two rows of three chairs, with space to walk between them. Player One stands at one end, Player Two at the other. P1's task is to correctly navigate the path *imagined* by P2, that brings P1 through the obstacles to P2. (The pattern exists only in the mind of P2, and may lead P1 through or around any chairs in the course.) The pattern should remain fairly simple. To aid P1, P2 may only *look* at P1. P2 may not under any circumstances make any gesture or facial movement. P2 may only provide a mental "yes" or "no" signal, to signify

P1's correct or incorrect direction. While making continuous eye contact with P2, P1 navigates the maze to P2. Afterward, P2 reveals how accurately P1 duplicated the pattern.

NOTES: 1. P2 may not make even the *slightest* squint or narrowing of facial features to P1. P2 must stay relaxed, and concentrate on transmitting only a vibration or feeling of "yes/no," "positive/negative," "light/dark," "right/wrong," etc.
2. P1 must also remain relaxed, and open to the *mood* he or she perceives from P2. They should move slowly, and may test and retest directions until they are satisfied that they are correct.

COMMENTS: Actors who know each other well, or have performed with each other for a long time, may find this easier than new partners. For this reason, be sure to mix new partners with old. Part of this exercise is to become aware of this connection, the other part is to practice cultivating it.

SPONTANEITY

*Spontaneity is the ability to summon an immediate, raw, unaltered creative impulse.*
The path to spontaneity is seen as a removal of mental and emotional blocks to the brain's natural abundance. The exercises that follow get the actors in touch with their own mental process. Once they can see and feel these processes at work in themselves, they can compare them to the common creative blocks described in the Spontaneity section of *The Art of Play*—the fear of judgment, the fear of failure, thinking without criteria, avoiding ambiguity, and others. As they identify them, they can begin to break through them using these exercises to *feel a conscious disconnection from their thoughts*. This is the primary focus of these exercises. Other exercises from the Free Association and Incorporation sections in Chapter Three further this process.

Spontaneity exercises are best performed just after trust exercises, early in the rehearsal day. As these exercises are explored, work to dispel the myths surrounding creative thought, and analyze common traps that trip up the improviser. This is the time actors must come to understand that there are differences and conflicts between our day-to-day cognition and creative thinking. The latter is dormant in most of us. We must find the "switch" so that when we enter creative time, we operate with the proper tools.

The director should distract the ensemble from personal expectations, and keep this a simple journey of experience (i.e., no self-judgment allowed!).

## Concentration

PURPOSE: To experience concentration.

DESCRIPTION: Players stand alone, facing a wall several feet away, and fix their focus on a speck or mark on the wall. After taking several deep breaths in through the nose and out through the mouth, players begin to practice letting all their awareness fall away, filling their minds only with the speck on the wall. Each time the player is aware of thinking, or of any unbidden thought, they are to relax, gently brush it out of their awareness, and refocus their attention on the speck, allowing it to absorb their consciousness completely. They are to watch the speck without thought or judgment, until the instructor calls a halt to the exercise.

NOTES: Players may be aided in clearing their minds at the start of the exercise by imagining a blank white screen, breathing deeply, then focusing on their speck.

COMMENTS: This exercise is an excellent precursor to the stream of consciousness exercise. It is also an excellent warm-up for performance. This exercise is actually a basic meditation technique, but it allows the actors to come to terms with, and learn to control, their own mental clarity and concentration. Players may not feel successful the first time this exercise is tried. It requires practice. Each time they should notice a better facility for controlling their thoughts.

## Stream of Consciousness

PURPOSE: To engage and experience the automatic nature of the mind. To flush out extraneous thoughts and anxieties, and learn the peculiarities of your own mind.

DESCRIPTION: Each player lies on the floor, arms to sides, legs flat, eyes closed. Players are asked to take several deep breaths and clear their minds. When instructed to begin, each player begins speaking in a continuous and unbroken stream of words. The words, phrases, or sounds must be audible, but need not make any syntactical sense. Players focus on releasing judgment of what they are saying until the words no longer seem like their own. They must resist the temptation to think or organize thoughts; any precognition must be released in favor of the unbidden and automatic. After five to seven minutes, the instructor ends the stream of consciousness.

NOTES: 1. Keep this exercise continuously verbal. This engages a different portion of the brain, and prevents players from experiencing a flood of images or thoughts that cannot be expressed in a linear fashion.
2. Actors should focus their attention, not on their thoughts and thinking, but on their mouths, and the sensations of forming the sounds.
3. Should players experience themselves *thinking* or judging what they are saying, remind them to simply relax, brush that awareness out of their conscious-ness, and refocus on *listening* to their stream.
4. The instructor may want to stop this exercise after the first few minutes, and discuss it briefly to be sure the players understand it correctly, then begin it again.
5. A stream of consciousness should not be an under-standable narrative (story). This points to a player who has not completely disengaged his or her con-scious mind.

COMMENTS: This exercise is chock full of good things. It can help actors learn the nature of their own mental processes and so learn to control them. It can put them directly in touch with the experience of spontaneity. It also makes a very valuable warm-up for performance, by allowing an actor to clear the mental cobwebs. Players will not necessarily experience a true stream of consciousness the first time they begin this exercise. It is one that needs to be repeated and practiced. When properly achieved, stream of consciousness sounds something like beat poetry, and it may feel completely foreign, as though someone else were speaking.

## Black Box

PURPOSE: To break established patterns of thought and behavior. To learn to accept the products of your imagination without judgment.

DESCRIPTION: The group divides into pairs, and sit facing each other. Player One guides Player Two through the following visualization: P2 is asked to relax, and to respond to all questions asked by P1 immediately and without judgment or reservation. P1 asks P2 to visualize a black box placed immediately in front of them. P2 describes it: size, shape, texture, etc. P2 lifts the lid and retrieves items from its darkness. At the bidding of P1, P2 describes the item's texture, shape, etc., then removes it for a visual inspection. P2 is not to think up responses, but first *perceives* the object in front of them, then describes what has been visualized without precognition. P1 continues to ask a fairly rapid series of questions aimed at *breaking up P2's normal patterns of thought*. For instance, if P2 retrieves a china figurine from the box, he or she may be asked to bite off a piece, chew it, describe what it tastes like, break it in half, see what is inside, hear its opinion, throw it into the air, see it explode and describe what rains down, etc. After several items and descriptive episodes, players switch roles.

NOTES:  1. The responding player must understand that this exercise is a perceptual journey, not a mental one. Questions should utilize all five senses.
   2. Responding players should be reminded that the questions may reveal something shocking or absurd, but that their imaginations will not harm them, and they should allow themselves to experience it without fear or judgment. (For instance, P1 might ask P2 to fire a visualized gun into his or her head, and to describe what comes out the other side, or to push it into his or her stomach and ask what flavor it is.)

COMMENTS: This exercise can really open actors up to spontaneous thought, and make them comfortable with their own imaginations. Be sure that the questions are asked fairly rapidly to keep the respondents off balance, and prevent them from thinking first. In this exercise sometimes chewing on a worm tastes like chewing on a worm, and sometimes it tastes like lemon drops. The players need to know that, either way, their response is perfectly acceptable.

## What Are You Doing?

PURPOSE: To practice spontaneously breaking mental context.

DESCRIPTION: Players stand in a circle facing inward, with adequate elbow room to either side. Player One begins a simple physical activity, such as chopping wood or brushing teeth. The player to the right, Player Two, asks P1, "What are you doing?" P1 is to answer immediately, with the first action that comes to mind *other than* the one he or she is doing. (For instance, going from "brushing my teeth" to "biting my nails" would not be as acceptable as going from "brushing my teeth" to "piloting a 747.") P2 then immediately begins the activity announced by P1. The player to P2's right, Player Three, asks, "What are you doing?" P2 then responds, and the process repeats around the circle. The group then breaks up and play in pairs.

NOTES: 1. Players must not think up their response in advance. They must keep their minds blank until the moment the question is asked, and then respond spontaneously.
2. The instructor should keep this exercise going at a swift pace to give players little time to think.
3. When the group is broken down into pairs, there is no time for the actor to prepare a response in advance!

## Automatic Reading

PURPOSE: To experience imagination visually.

DESCRIPTION: One player sits in a relaxed position, breathes deeply, and clears his or her mind. The instructor brings them through a guided visualization where the player stands at a bookcase, chooses, then removes one book. The players are to respond only to their automatic visual impressions. They are not to "think," they are merely to describe what they *see*. They first describe the cover in detail (e.g., color, texture, age), then open to a page and read the page number in the top right-hand corner. The instructor suggests there is a poem written on the page, and asks the player to read the title. They read the first word of the first line, then the second word, then the first line, second line, etc., to the end of the poem. Another player writes down the poem as it is read, so that it may be read back later. Large groups may split into groups of three and play among themselves.

NOTES: If players cannot visualize or seem to be thinking up answers, have them take a deep breath, refocus, and go back to describing the cover, or get a new book. Have them describe the physical detail of the book as far as they are able (e.g., thickness, weight, smell, color, decoration), then gradually work them into reading the text.

COMMENTS: When players are fully relaxed and focused, the poems they read automatically may be remarkably coherent. Often meter and rhyme are fully in place, and the poem itself makes sense. The player will often feel no connection whatever to the content of the poem, as though it were written by someone else. This exhibits their connection with the deeper levels of thought.

## Automatic Writing

PURPOSE: To experience spontaneity through writing.

DESCRIPTION: Each member of the group has a blank sheet of paper and a pencil. They take several deep breaths to relax and clear their minds, then proceed as in the Stream of Consciousness exercise, except that instead of verbalizing, they write.

NOTES:  1. Just as the players absorb themselves with oral sensations in the Stream of Consciousness exercise, in this exercise, they absorb themselves with the tactile feeling of writing.
2. When the automatic engages, players should feel as though they are watching someone else's hand write.
3. Players should not be concerned with whether their writing makes syntactical sense, is spelled correctly, or whether it forms words, scribbles, or designs.
4. Coach players to *Let your minds go! Release your judgment! Let your hands do the writing! Feel the words coming out through your hand!*

COMMENTS: This exercise also takes some practice. Players may at first find only brief moments of true automatic writing. Attempt this exercise only after the group is well warmed up. Players seem to find it more effective when attempting this exercise at the end of rehearsals when they are more fatigued, because they are less likely to expend the energy to judge.

## Period Style Workshops

Period style workshops include dialect training, language, history, customs, manners, and movement. Start this specialized training in the first phase of rehearsals and continue it throughout. It is most effective to present a short workshop each day, rather than fewer longer ones, because repetition over a longer period of time helps actors to internalize the information.

Remember it is not enough that they be able to accurately reproduce the elements of style in a workshop; they must do so automatically and spontaneously in their character improv. There is more than teaching involved here. It is also a matter of *conditioning*. These workshops should be as active as possible. They may even be integrated into character development or improv workshops later in rehearsals. (See Chapter Eight of *The Art of Play*.)

### DIALECT TRAINING

Classic dialect training, as would be used for any period stage play, is appropriate here. Some attempt at dialect training should be made no matter how close to modern day the period is. Delineating the actor from the guest is very important. The closer one gets to modern day, the harder that becomes.

The pronounced changes in vowel sounds among different nationalities and different centuries are great when they exist. But periods of this century don't always have them. For periods such as the 1920s, '40s, even the '50s, '60s, or '80s, differences in vocal inflection and cadence can be remarkably distinct. Sound recordings, records, newsreels, television, and films offer plenty of resource material for these dialectic subtleties.

For interactive events, where the complement of characters spans the social spectrum, break dialects down into two or three social classes, e.g., upper, middle, lower. This simplifies the problem of presenting the dialects of an entire range of society, and still gives the impression to the guest that all different walks of life are present.

LANGUAGE

Language is as important as dialect. Language involves the lexicon of the characters and how they structure their speech. This is rarely an issue in stage work because the playwright has already provided the language, but for interactive theatre it is an absolute necessity.

One begins by separating the vocabulary of the period that is not used in modern speech. The instructor prepares a vocabulary glossary, listing every antique or slang expression they can possibly find. Literature offers a great source for such a list. If you are doing a Dickens festival, read Charles Dickens; if you're doing a Renaissance festival, read through an annotated Shakespeare anthology. For 1940s Hollywood characters I gleaned my list from historical references, films and radio of the '40s, and books on American slang.

In the same vein, a listing of epithets, or common expressions, should be made. Expressions for love, insults, curses, and jubilation abound in every period. These usually reek of the period and can be used in many situations.

Beyond vocabulary, determine how words were used that are unique to that period. Some periods used metaphor more than others; some used verbs as nouns; some, like the English Renaissance, used different sentence construction, different syntax and grammar, etc. Others use repetitive hooks or phrases such as the 1960s' "man" ("Nice car, man!"), or the 1940s' "say" ("Say, that's some car!"). Isolate as many stylistic differences as you can, teach them, then have the cast use them until they speak it in their sleep.

Here are a few language exercises I have used over time to help actualize vocabulary, syntax, and grammar.

## Character Letters

PURPOSE: To become familiar with the vocabulary and syntax of a period language.

DESCRIPTION: The cast writes a one-page letter from their character to whomever they choose, based on a topic or attitude given by the instructor, such as a love letter, a complaint, or a thank-you. In the letter, they are to use any materials at their disposal to incorporate as much as they can of the vocabulary, syntax, grammar, and style of the language to be used in the production. The letters are then read aloud to the group. The letters should be consistent with their characterization and the context of the production, although they may involve fictitious characters or information from their character's background.

COMMENTS: There is a great advantage to composing and writing out the period language. The act of writing not only helps the memory, but its incorporation into the character's reality helps as well. In addition, the reading of the letters aloud to the group is an excellent language review for everyone, and also helps the group to a greater understanding of fellow characters.

## Telephone Slang Conversation

PURPOSE: To develop period vocabulary.

DESCRIPTION: Two characters are seated in chairs faced away from each other, as though presenting a split scene of two people talking on the telephone. (This can be done whether or not the telephone was invented during the period of the production.) Actors may have in their laps any vocabulary list compiled for rehearsals, and may refer to it freely during the conversation. Characters begin their conversation and incorporate as many vocabulary words and phrases as they possibly can.

COMMENTS: Several of these scenes can be set up at the same time for the sake of time and practice. Depending on where you are in the rehearsal process, this may be done in character or out.

## Slang Conversation Translation

PURPOSE: Practice translating modern speech into period language.

DESCRIPTION: Two chairs are placed side by side in the performance space, facing the group. Players One through Four are called to the stage. P1 and P2 are seated in the chairs, P3 stands behind P1, and P4 stands behind P2. P3 and P4, standing, are given a character relationship and a conflict for their conversation. They are playing modern characters and need not act out the action of the scene, but remain behind their chairs as they converse with each other. For instance, a character relationship may be mother-daughter, and the conflict may be dating the wrong fella. P1 and P2 are to translate the conversation into period speech, and may refer to vocabulary notes if the instructor allows. P3 begins by speaking a line of dialogue to P4, P1 translates P3's line of dialogue using period speech. P4 responds to that line of dialogue as his or her modern character, then P2 translates P4's line into period speech, and so on. The conversation continues until the instructor calls a halt. Actors may then switch roles and new variables be given for the next scene.

NOTES:  1. The conversation works best if a heated debate is established, and translators translate with little or no hesitation.
2. Speakers may challenge their translators by using modern slang and colloquialisms, but must also add new information to keep the conversation interesting.

COMMENTS: The act of translating helps to separate the two languages in the mind of the speaker. It will help to slow down their otherwise automatic reactions in modern speech.

## Merchants

PURPOSE: To break out of conditioned linguistic patterns, by being required to speak with the exclusion of certain words.

DESCRIPTION: Groups of four or five players choose among them a *merchant*. This merchant chooses what he/she will sell to the rest of the group. The merchant tells the group the name of the item to be sold before the exercise begins. The merchant is timed for two minutes and in that time tries to sell each member of the group, one at a time. To sell a player, the merchant must, during the course of discussion, get the player to say either the *name of the item* being sold, or the words "yes," "no," or "I." When the merchant's time is up, another player is chosen to be merchant, and a new item chosen. The exercise is over when all players have played the merchant. The merchant with the lowest time to sell all in the group, or the greatest number of group members sold, is the best merchant.

NOTES:  1. Once a player is *sold* (makes an incorrect response),

the merchant moves immediately to the next player and continues to sell.
2. Remind merchants to get the player to respond *as often as possible.* The longer the *merchant* talks, the less opportunity the *player* will have to trip up!

COMMENTS: This is an old parlor game. Merchants will find many devious ways to trip up their opponents. This exercise is lots of fun, as well as a very useful way of getting actors to think and speak outside of their comfortable patterns. This is useful when trying to establish new patterns.

## Crambo

PURPOSE: Practice in focusing on specific descriptive language. Practice thinking and speaking outside normal patterns.

DESCRIPTION: The group pairs up. Player One chooses silently a word that is easily rhymed, such as "day," "cat," or "house." The object is for Player Two to guess the secret word. P1 gives P2 a word that *rhymes* with the secret word. (For instance, if the secret word is "nickel," P1 may give the word "pickle".) P2 then makes a guess, but phrases the guess without saying the actual word. For example, if P2 guesses the word "sickle" for the given rhyme "pickle," he/she might say, "Is it the sharp knife at the end of a pole the farmer uses to harvest his crop?" If P2 is not correct, P1 says so, and gives another rhyme of the secret word, but this time, and from then on, P1 must also phrase it without saying the actual word. For example, to give the new clue word "tickle," P1 would say, "What I do when I wiggle my finger under your armpit." Play continues until the secret word is guessed. Variation 1: Choose only verbs and have players enact the guesses. Variation 2: Play can be conducted in two groups, as is done in charades.

COMMENTS: We become so used to some words that we take their meaning for granted. This exercise helps the actor to be specific and deliberate in their use of language.

HISTORY WORKSHOP

A knowledge of the period's history is essential in conveying that period in performance. Contrary to what might be assumed, actors need not each be scholars of the period's history, but must indeed have a solid working knowledge of what their *character* would know—specifically, what the character would need to know in the pursuit of his or her occupation and in the day-to-day business of life. This limits the burden of total scholarship to an area of expertise—much simpler to accomplish in a four- to six-week rehearsal period. Here is what each character needs to know about the period:

- *Major current events that would be common knowledge to that character.* Remember, before the days of radio and television, or even print, people's knowledge of the world was far more limited. Sometimes what a character does not know can be as revealing as what they do know. Also, they would know these events only within the context of their previous knowledge; they do not have the historic hindsight that we do.
- *Knowledge specific to their occupational activity.* This is perhaps the most important area for the actor, because they will be using it most often. Their understanding here should be the most detailed; they are the company experts on their occupation. From the guest's point of view, a vast amount of historic information will be encountered from their collective associations with character occupations.
- *Everyday knowledge common to all in the period.* Categories may include currency and prices of things; transportation; recreation; art, music, and literature; fashion; health and hygiene; government and justice; industry; technology and inventions; religion; superstition; holidays; family life, marriage, gender roles, child rearing; and education.
- *Cultural attitudes, values, and beliefs.* Every period has its own world view. The way people thought about themselves, each other, and the world and their place in it differs for every age—even every decade. These attitudes, values, and beliefs define who we are, and are therefore critical in any depiction of the past. Outline the important cultural suppositions of the time, and have the cast play them out. Some may seem wrong or uncomfortable to the actors' ways of thinking. Remind them that they are not portraying themselves, and that their personal attitudes do not come into play for their role. The actor must discard their views in favor of the character's. They must embrace and enjoy whatever values the character has.

*History Bible* ■ Historical reference information should be prepared for the actor before rehearsal begins. During preproduction research, a "history bible" should be compiled. This is a collection of only the most useful, playable historic information. This "actional information" is information relating to the period that can be *made evident in the characters' activities within the performance environment*. The bible boils down information into bite-size chunks the actors can easily digest during rehearsals. This not only economizes on the actor's time, but provides an important step in getting the information from the actor's head into the performance.

One of my instructors at the Sterling Renaissance Festival devised a very clever exercise to make the tidbits of history from the bible come alive for the cast. He would first instruct a few members of the group in staging throughout the performance environment small scenes that exemplify certain aspects of history he wanted to make clear. He would then take the rest of the cast on a guided tour of a day in the life of the space, and let these scenes take the cast by surprise. In making the performance space his own living history park, he was able to give the cast a visceral feel for the period. It was also a lot of fun, and gave the cast a taste of what being a guest is like.

## Guided Dream in Character

PURPOSE: To create a sense memory awareness of the time period presented in the production.

DESCRIPTION: Participants begin by finding a comfortable place on the floor, and lie flat with their arms to their sides. The first part of this exercise involves participants relaxing their bodies and minds, in preparation for the sensory journey. They are first asked to take deep breaths, in through the nose and out through the mouth. The instructor leads them through a visualization of relaxing each part of their body, by imagining a warm beam of sunlight melting the tension away. As the light travels along the body, from toe to head, each body part is relaxed in order: feet, ankles, calves, thighs, hips, torso, chest, back, upper arms, lower arms, hands, neck, head, face, jaw, and finally throat. Throughout this relaxation section, they are asked to visualize a field of pure white, and to gently brush aside any distracting thoughts that enter their consciousness. In addition, as each body part is relaxed, they are to forget about it, as though it were not even there; they may even visualize it turning to dust and blowing away on a warm breeze. The instructor reminds them periodically to continue breathing deeply, and that although they are relaxed, their minds must remain aware and awake. In this relaxed and receptive state, the second part of the exercise begins.

The instructor tells them to allow their imaginations to bring them back to the time period presented in the production. The instructor now begins a narrative that takes the actor on a walking journey, from outside the environment to that environment, and through it. They begin their journey by discovering themselves by a roadside. They examine their clothing and surroundings, then begin walking toward their goal. The narrative may take whatever shape the instructor chooses, but should allow them to experience the historical setting with all five senses. In general, the characters' journey toward the environment acquaints them along the way with several of that world's residents, and leads them to experience the real environment depicted in the production. Along the way their encounters may be happy, sad, fascinating, fearful, poignant, etc. The narrative should always end with the character happy and content, in the company of good friends in celebration and laughter. The exercise concludes with the scene fading to the field of white. Actors are told that they are now fully aware, awake, and themselves once again, and may sit up when ready.

NOTES:  1. The instructor must emphasize to actors that they must concentrate their focus on their awareness and not allow themselves to become sleepy.
2. The instructor should emphasize detail, but allow each traveler to experience it in their own way. To this end, pauses should be inserted into the narrative, e.g., "*A figure moves toward you.* (pause) *It is a wizened old man who begs a favor.* (pause) *You grant his request and move down the road.* (pause) *You pause to smell the scent in the breeze,* (pause) *and take in the colors of the forest"* (pause).
3. Actors should allow themselves to be whomever their imagination suggests, and it is best for this exercise for them not to play their characters.

COMMENTS: This exercise will leave a powerful and lasting sense-memory impression of the period being depicted. It may also enhance the character's sense of belonging to the environment, and solidify the actor's emotional relationship to his or her character. You may wish to repeat it later in rehearsals. I always end this exercise with the group of friends getting silly drunk in their celebration, a joke told by one is bungled so badly it makes the traveler unable to stop laughing, then the look of concern in the traveler's friends' faces makes him or her laugh all the harder, and so on. If told properly, this Möbius loop of laughing about laughing usually gets the entire room in hysterics.

## Character Letters—Variation I

PURPOSE: Practice in incorporating period language, history, and values into a narrative.

DESCRIPTION: Each actor in the group writes a one-page "letter," although it may be any type of narrative form, e.g., conversation, speech, even inner thoughts. It must, however, be the character speaking. At the instructor's discretion, a certain number of period vocabulary words, historical facts or references, and period values must be incorporated into the narrative. (For instance: six period words or expressions, three historic references, and one period value.) Each actor reads their letter aloud to the group.

It is most effective to continue this exercise on a daily basis. I often present one or the other of these *letter exercises* as "homework," and begin each style workshop with the reading of them.

CUSTOMS, MANNERS, AND MOVEMENT

Actions and movement can often be unique to a historic period. My Renaissance performers, for instance, learn the proper way of bowing or presenting oneself to the opposite sex and the proper way to address the various classes. Many subcultures have their own ways, even secret languages. Upper-class Elizabethan ladies used their fans to signal cues to their suitors; the thieves of London had their own language they called "canting" or "peddler's French." Postures and movements indicated social station, and often revealed what the people of the time considered beautiful. A study of these items should be a part of any style workshop.

One excellent source for rehearsing period style is *Style for Actors* by Robert Barton. It includes a "styles checklist" that supplies all the questions an actor needs to ask in order to get inside the head of a period character.

## *Attractions Rehearsals*

Most performance elements can't be rehearsed until characterizations are firm, and so must be started later in the process. Anything that can be rehearsed before the characters are developed should be started at the opening of the rehearsal process, and then give way to more character-based elements as characters become firm. This, of course, includes any attractions. Attractions are shows within the show, such as stunts, dancing, singing, and theatrical performances. In this way, each rehearsal day includes both workshops and rehearsals. In the early phases, attractions rehearsals are held, and gradually give way to encounter and scenario rehearsals.

Often the special talents of the actor can be used to create attractions during this time. If an actor sings, give him/her a song; if they dance, create a period dance; if they play a period instrument, give them music to learn. Any special ability, be it physical comedy, stage combat, or juggling, may be useful in creating an attraction.

# *Preparation* 3
# *Phase*

As Freeing the Imagination workshops, Styles workshops, and attractions rehearsals continue, define
the performance elements and outline the choices
to be made in character development.

Describe interactive theatre as an invitation to the guest
to return to play. Explain that the art of interactive performance is in teaching and *coaxing* the guest to explore and
contribute to the theatrical reality through spontaneous creativity. (See Chapters Two and Three of *The Art of Play.*)

## *Discovery of Performance Elements*

If you are rehearsing actors who have no prior knowledge
of interactive performance, their first question will be "What
is the *show*?" or "What do I *do*?" This is their desire for
structure speaking. Use this time to lay out the mechanics,
if you will, of interactive performance so that they have a
context to focus upon. This is important because it won't be
until late in the rehearsal process that these elements are
developed; this is too long for actors to be in suspense
about what their performance will entail. Use lecture spar-
ingly in this; emphasize discussion, anecdote, and example.

*49*

Describe interactive performance as a *combination of perfor-mance structures* they will use either *randomly* or on a *scheduled basis*. Describe how the subject, environment, themes, and charac-ters interrelate in your production, and point out the interactive genre's shift in emphasis from *story* to *character* in relating the themes of the show. (See Chapters Four and Five of *The Art of Play*.)

Reveal to the cast, at least in general terms, the principles of the performance elements: endowments, character action, lazzi, conceitti, encounters, and scenarios (see Chapter Fifteen of *The Art of Play*). Don't get bogged down in the details of performing these elements here; there is time for that in later phases. It is enough that a basic understanding is established, to focus the actors' intent and let them know what is beyond the improv and character development work they are now embarking upon.

If you are rehearsing an interactive play, describe these ele-ments as *revolving around a master scenario* that tells the story. Explain how plot points in the master scenario *anchor the story in a conventional way*, but the performance elements *define the details for each performance*. Earmark for them the date work begins on the master scenario. This is the closest thing they will have to a script, so they will want to set their sights on it.

## Discovery of Character Elements

The director should keep discussion on character elements as active as possible; make it more discovery than discussion. Try to keep the actors out of their heads; let them actively experience each concept before moving on to the next. Remind them to trust the process.

Here, as in every step of development, the actors are in com-plete control of their choices. Actors must understand that they have both the freedom and the responsibility to make the choices that *work for them*. They also must understand that they have free rein to change their minds up to the point the director requires them to commit. Even from that point, their choices will develop and grow for as long as they play the character.

### ESSENTIAL QUALITIES OF CHARACTER

Before diving into the building process of interactive characteri-zation, spend some time clarifying the *outcome* of that process. What are the qualities that a finished character must have to be successful? It only makes sense to give the actors a clear picture of what they are after before they begin creating it. These six essential qualities—extraordinary, fascinating, identifiable, approachable, vulnerable, and likable—form the litmus test of the character's interactive *aptitude* (see Chapter Six of *The Art of Play*). Together they form the *common nature* of all interactive characterizations. The exercises below will help to warm the actor to this common nature.

*Extraordinary* ■ Define the extraordinary as "extra-ordinary," or "outside the ordinary," narrowing the definition to *that which is condensed and intensified from real life*. This supplies the larger-than-life quality and action of the character, and makes it *theatrical*. The exercise below will get actors more in touch with the quality of the extraordinary. Emphasize the importance of a character being magnified but proportional to real life, and not falling into caricature. Explain how this can reduce a character's believability, and warn against it.

## Extraordinary Characters

PURPOSE: To connect the actor with the extraordinary, and observe how that quality is revealed.

DESCRIPTION: Actors are asked to think of an extraordinary character that they know from real life, not one from the stage, (e.g., a friend, relative, professor, stranger, anyone at all that they have observed themselves). They are asked to examine what makes that character extraordinary—their posture, movements, rhythms, gestures, idiosyncrasies, vocal qualities, mannerisms—every aspect of that person that stands *out of the ordinary*. One at a time, they get up and perform that character for the group, revealing what they think is extraordinary about them. After the portrayal, and some brief observations from the group on what they think made the character extraordinary and memorable, the actor is allowed to give their backstory on the person.

NOTES: Discuss what made that character extraordinary; *focus on the details*. Ask the performer what they thought was extraordinary about this person, and how they chose to reveal it.

COMMENTS: Sometimes these are fairly ordinary people with just one extraordinary element to them; sometimes they're

complete whackos. Seeing this pageant of extraordinary characters really connects the company with that feeling of the extraordinary. It is all the more poignant when they know they are
real people.

## Extraordinary Story

PURPOSE: To better relate to condensed action.

DESCRIPTION: This is a storytelling exercise where each actor
relates their best true-life tall tale. As each one is related, guide
the group's attention toward how tightly packed the key action
is, and how fate or chance intervenes to create a string of
events that are well out of the norm. Actors usually become
quite absorbed in this exercise. I prompt them to explain why
they are absorbed, and to describe their source of pleasure.

COMMENTS: After this, it is easier for an actor to relate to the
idea of their character living always in a theatrical economy of
action. I conclude by announcing that all of the extraordinary
events they have just heard are the "norm" for their characters'
activity in performance.

*Fascinating* ■  This deals with a character's ability to capture
and hold the interest of the audience. Fascination draws them in.
To fascinate, a character answers questions that only raise new
ones; it is a tantalizing mixture of revelation and mystery. Actors
should develop a characterization that fascinates *them*. Explore
specific ways a character may fascinate an audience. You may
often draw examples from material presented in the
Extraordinary Character and Extraordinary Story exercises.

*Identifiable* ■  The quality of identifiability is equated directly
with character exposition in a conventional play. Make plain the
need for the audience to have a sense of foreknowledge about
*who the character is* before comfortable interaction can take
place. Lay out techniques on how an actor may telegraph the key
elements of characterization from a distance, i.e., before
approaching the guest.

## Emotions at a Distance

PURPOSE: To practice magnifying physicality and telegraphing emotion or attitude.

DESCRIPTION: Characters line up at one end of a large open space (thirty to forty yards is best). Player One goes to the opposite end, having previously been given a secret emotion. At that distance, he or she physically expresses that emotion. The group tries to guess what that emotion could be. Once guessed correctly, that actor returns, and another actor is sent out with an emotion to display. The same may be done for attitudes.

COMMENTS: It is often surprising how large and precise an actor must be in order to reveal an emotion from that distance.

The following exercises may be done as a series. They can help get the actor in touch with being *emotionally evident.* You may repeat these exercises in-character when developing the character's physicality (during Development of Semblance).

## Attitude Stills

PURPOSE: To explore making attitudes clear and identifiable.

DESCRIPTION: Players mill and seethe about the rehearsal space as the instructor calls out attitudes. (An attitude is the position or posture assumed by the body in connection with one's disposition, opinion, or mental set, such as superiority, disdain, or admiration.) As each attitude is called out, actors are to immediately stop and strike that attitudinal pose. Actors are still, but not "frozen." After a brief moment of holding the pose, the instructor allows them to continue milling and seething, before calling out the next attitude.

NOTES: Actors are to strive for clarity, such that an observer would be able to easily name the attitude without hearing it called out.

## Attitude Pairs

PURPOSE: To further explore and clarify attitudes.

DESCRIPTION: The full group breaks up into pairs. Players One and Two stand facing each other in neutral body positions. The instructor calls out a pair of opposing attitudes, such as "admiration" and "disdain," or "timid" and "aggressive." P1 acquires the first attitude in the pair, P2 the second. They immediately strike *no-motion* poses (not freezes), and hold them until they are as clear as possible. The instructor then tells them to slowly acquire their partner's attitude, stressing that the transition must be slow and deliberate. They then switch back *slowly*. The instructor then calls for them to switch attitudes *immediately*, then back and forth a few times. Players are then asked to work together to motivate their shifts in attitudes. For instance, a timid attitude can be motivated by a threatening gesture, while an aggressive attitude can be motivated by flinching as if to be struck.

NOTES:  1. Coach actors to use their whole bodies in defining their attitudes.
2. Actors are not to converse but to communicate through attitude and gesture only.

## Attitude Scenes

PURPOSE: Exploring clarity and shifting attitudes within a scene.

DESCRIPTION: **Part I**: Players One and Two are given contrasting attitudes, and play a scene. During this scene they must motivate an exchange of attitudes. (P2 acquires P1's; P1 acquires P2's.) They then motivate a shift back to their original attitudes, and close the scene.

**Part II**: P1 and 2 proceed as before, except that they are given their attitudes in private so that each is unaware of the other's attitude. Players are not allowed to state their attitudes within the scene, but must make them clear through their actions and behavior. The scene begins, and at the point where both actors are certain that each knows the other's attitude, they motivate the shift in attitudes as before. They then shift again, to their original attitudes, and close the scene. After, actors try to guess the exact word given to describe their partner's attitude.

NOTES: Once attitudes are switched, they must hold them until both are sure that the transaction is completed.

COMMENTS: In addition to teaching actors how to be clear in their attitudes, this exercise also teaches the importance of an emotional level in scene work.

*Approachable* ■ Demonstrate that approachability is an essential factor in breaking down the guest's inhibitions and personal defense mechanisms. Give examples on how approachability affects audience behavior. Outline (or observe through the exercise below) techniques for engendering approachability in a character.

## Approachability Postures

PURPOSE: To examine how approachability is manifested in character.

DESCRIPTION: This is simply an exercise where an actor shows a character that is unapproachable, and as a group we examine the details of that character to discover what makes it appear unapproachable. Likewise, we then show characters that are approachable, and examine them in the same way.

*Vulnerable* ■ When characters show a weakness, usually through their foible, they take on a vulnerability that makes them less threatening to the guest. Describe how vulnerability can disarm a perceived control issue with the guest and lead to better interactive encounters.

## Vulnerable Person Exercise

PURPOSE: To explore the qualities of vulnerability.

DESCRIPTION: Each player, in turn, enters the space alone, and reveals a *vulnerable personality*. After all, or several, players have performed, the instructor guides the group in a discussion about what made the characters seem vulnerable.

NOTES: Ask to see as many different types of vulnerability as the cast is able to present. Examine each for the quality that makes them vulnerable. Define vulnerability as a *lack of defense*.

COMMENTS: This exercise should get the cast in touch with characterizations that are open and approachable. You will see both positive forms of vulnerability (as in innocence), and negative forms of vulnerability (as in fear). Point out that the more positive aspects of being vulnerable are what is required of the interactive character.

*Likable*   ■   Finally, suggest that characters must *approve of the guest and of themselves*, whether or not the character is "good" or "bad."

ELEMENTS OF CHARACTERIZATION

Here lay out the building blocks of interactive characterization. Walk through the process, and help the actor understand *why* each block is chosen and *how* each fits with the others.

Chapter Seven of *The Art of Play* outlines the development process in its proper order and in great detail. It makes an excellent reference. Whether the entire process is presented before work begins, or whether it is revealed during the process is a matter of directorial preference. I like to do a little of both: characterize it in general terms so that actors understand how elements relate, but keep them most keenly focused on the current element. The process should flow in this order:

1. *Define occupation and theme.* This may be a given in most productions, but the actor can refine it. Occupation is what the character does more than anything else, and may or may not have anything to do with their livelihood. It is their strongest *actional* quality in support of the subject of the production. The theme is the idea or underlying motif we see developed or elaborated by the character. Themes are the facets of human nature revealed by what is suggested by the subject. Each character exploits one theme.
2. *Create occupational activities.* Compile a list of *quintessential actions, duties, and behaviors* commonly assumed to be a part of the occupation. This (long) list is to be composed without any regard for the appropriateness of the activity to the actor's precepts, or even their playability within the performance environment. It is a palette of possible actions only, and will widen the actor's scope of choices.
3. *Refine the occupational activities.* Narrow the occupational activities list to usable choices based on the following three

criteria: (1) they reveal the character's theme; (2) they require interaction with others for their accomplishment; (3) they can actually be performed in the performance environment.

4. *Choose the character's passion.* Make this important choice that is at the core of the character. Define the single state of being that will bring the character to final happiness. (e.g., to be approved by others, to be respected, to be in control, to be loved, etc.) Define also the motivating origin of this passionate desire. This gives the character a slant towards how it will reveal its theme.

5. *Define the character's foible.* Identify the comic flaw that trips the character up in his or her attempts to achieve his or her passion and creates the internal conflict. Choose also the motivating origin of the foible.

6. *Define the character's virtue.* The virtue undoes the fault of the foible and places the character back on the road to passion fulfillment.

7. *Identify primary needs.* The character's *primary needs* are those two or three needs that most directly serve the attainment of the passion. They should indicate the types of activities the character will engage in most often.

8. *Identify primary activities.* Work through the refined occupational activities list and choose the eight to ten activities that *best answer the primary needs, reveal the character's particular slant on his or her theme, and provide the most expansive range of action.* The character has an urgent and intense need to perform these activities. These are the activities the character will most often use in performance.

As actors make discoveries and decisions about their characters, have them record them on paper. Careful character notes prevent the actor's concepts from drifting over time and becoming vague. This may seem improbable to the actor—"How could I forget my own character?"—but it happens. There is a big difference between a character developing over time and one that just becomes vague. Growth is good, but actors must be able to refer back to where they started in order to know where they have come.

Understanding these character elements is part of this phase (Preparation phase); developing them is part of the next phase (Choices phase) and continues into the following phase (Development phase). The movement from one phase to the next should be guided by each cast's progress, but the material in these phases provides an orderly set of tools to bring them through the process with clarity. The following exercise is one tool that can help the actor see how these elements fit together to form a character.

## Group-Created Character

PURPOSE: To see the process of character creation without the burden of self-judgment that accompanies the actor using his or her own character's choices.

DESCRIPTION: In the form of a group discussion led by the instructor, the group creates a full set of elements for a fictitious character. The instructor writes choices on a large pad or blackboard. Use an occupation different from any in the cast, but applicable to the same production. Identify occupational activities and narrow them; choose a passion and its origin, foibles and their origins, virtues, primary needs, then primary activities. Afterward, various members of the group get up and give their interpretations of the character.

NOTES:   1. It is often useful to have a number of actors prepare their creations separately so that different approaches to the same set of elements can be viewed.
2. Examine how each actor chose to physicalize the elements and how their creations measure up to the essential qualities of characterization.

COMMENTS: Use this exercise when actors are sketchy about how the elements fit together. It doesn't matter if the characterization is flawed; it will serve as a great example for what *not* to do without having to refer to an actual character. Point out that in a group-created character, choices do not have the advantage of one individual's unique creative vision.

*Character Development Lists* ■   Actors can use the Occupational Activities List that follows to record their raw activities list and its successive refinements. The Character Elements List on page 59 provides a place for actors to record their character choices as identified above.

## Occupational Activities List

**Actor's Name** _____

**Production** _____

**Role** _____

**Character's Name** _____

**Character's Occupation** _____

**Occupational Activities That Reveal the Subject**

1. _____

⬇ _____

_____

100. _____


## Character Elements List

**Name** _____

**Role** _____

**Occupation** _____

**Character Theme** _____

**Passion** _____

    Origin _____

    _____

    _____

**Foible** _____

    Origin _____

    _____

    _____

**Virtue** _____

**Primary Activities** (Activities key to passion fulfillment, and performed most often)

1. _____

2. _____

3. _____

4._____

5._____

6._____

7._____

8._____

9._____

10._____

**Primary Needs** (Based on primary activities, and in order of importance to the character)

1._____

2._____

3._____

## Freeing the Imagination Continues

### FREE-ASSOCIATION

*What the mind perceives, the mind associates.*
This continuation of the Freeing the Imagination workshop deals with the natural associative abilities of the mind, and how our need for criteria makes us selective in our thinking. (See Chapter Eleven of *The Art of Play*.) Although separated by a chapter in this book, there should be a seamless transition from Spontaneity to Free Association.

Once actors have a grasp on the creative traps we set for ourselves and have acquired a visceral connection to the feel of spontaneous thought, they may begin the practice of free association. I say "practice" because we are literally burning new engrams in the brain, to shake the tenacious hold selectivity has on our creative thought process. Burn, baby, burn!

Directors would be wise to emphasize at this point that we are exercising *components* of the creative process here *in isolation*, in order to first understand them, then bring them together later in a clearer and more fortified way. Any attempt to relate the function of one of these components to the improvised scene will fail, as comparing a crankshaft to a drive to the store will fail—there's no obvious connection until the whole story is told. Just get them to focus on free-associating with confidence, joy, and ease.

## Word Association

PURPOSE: To experience the associative process of the mind.
DESCRIPTION: The group pairs up. Players seat themselves facing each other. Player One gives Player Two a random word. P2 responds with the first word that comes to mind. P1 then uses that word to immediately associate yet another word. Players continue word association as swiftly as possible.

NOTES: Coach actors to relax, not to judge, and to associate with *only* the previous word.

COMMENTS: This exercise is unlike what you might be given by Sigmund Freud, because the words being associated have no direction or purpose, as they would have if a psychiatrist were providing them. Each player is associating from the word before it, so it is an association-association relationship. It will create a stream of words, which will take a wild and far-flung course. The key here is to associate freely and immediately.

## Word Ball

PURPOSE: To practice spontaneity and free association with a time constraint.

DESCRIPTION: The group stands in a circle of six to ten players facing inward. An invisible ball is swiftly and randomly tossed, underhand, from one to another across the circle. When tossing, players must first make eye contact with their intended receiver. When players are comfortable with the physicalization of throwing the invisible ball, the instructor asks them to shout out a word as they toss the ball. The word must be *summoned automatically* at the instant the imaginary ball leaves the fingers of the tosser. Before that time, the tosser's mind must be relaxed and free of any precognition. As each player catches the ball, they are also catching the word thrown with it. This word alone is the *flash* for their next word. The instructor may later add the element of each player expressing an attitude while throwing their word. It can also be played with only three players, to increase the frequency of required responses.

NOTES: As players catch the word ball, they are to concentrate on absorbing the word as it is caught, then *follow* their mind's

instant associative response. Coach players: *Don't prethink! Let the word happen as it leaves your fingers! Let go! Relax! Rely on your spontaneity! Know that any word is the right word!*
COMMENTS: This exercise is always good practice, but it is simple enough to do in the earliest stages of rehearsal. If players get sloppy with throwing their ball, you can substitute a real ball, one that can be easily caught.

## Image Association

PURPOSE: To explore how visual images spark associated images.

DESCRIPTION: The group pairs up. Partners sit on the floor facing each other. Both players close their eyes. Player One expresses a visual image to Player Two using one sentence or phrase. P2 is to perceive the very next image that comes to mind and relate that visual image to P1 in one short phrase. This exercise is played like the Word Association exercise, except that full visual images are used. Players are not to anticipate or judge their images.

NOTES:  1. Players are to associate with the previous image only, not the collective string of images before it. Once an image is associated, it is then forgotten in favor of the next. If players have difficulty expressing their whole image, they may describe its most prominent element.
2. Coach players to *Describe the first image! Use one simple phrase! Relay only visual images, not emotional feelings! Trade "pictures"! Don't pause, keep it moving!*

COMMENTS: Practicing this visual flash can be very beneficial. Players will share experiences of the associations taking on a particular pattern, but if they follow a narrative form, this may suggest that the player is prethinking or stringing together previous images.

## Image Ball

PURPOSE: To experience the associative process under time constraint.

DESCRIPTION: Image Ball proceeds just as the Word Ball exercise, except that instead of a word, a visual image is passed.

NOTES: Images must be described quickly as the image ball is tossed, a few words only.

COMMENTS: Once the group is comfortable with associating images, Image Ball is a good exercise to effect that association on cue. Image Ball, like Word Ball, can be played with only two players to increase the frequency of required responses.

## The Minister's Cat

PURPOSE: To experience the associative process within pre-scribed criteria. To learn to relax and concentrate under pressure.

DESCRIPTION: Groups of no more than ten stand in a circle facing each other. One player begins a rhythm by slapping both hands on his/her thighs. He/she then begins the exercise by repeating these words in rhythm: "The minister's cat is a (blank) cat," filling in the blank with a word that begins with the letter A. The player to the right must repeat the phrase without breaking the rhythm, adding a new word to the blank, also beginning with the letter A. This process continues around the circle, with each player adding a different word beginning with the same letter. If a player falters in the rhythm or repeats a word previously spoken, the play stops and that player is excluded from the game. The play begins again with the player to the right, using a word for the blank beginning with the next letter in the alphabet. As each player makes a mistake and is excluded, the letters proceed through the alphabet, A, B, C, etc. The exercise is over when only one player is left. To increase the difficulty, smaller groups or pairs of players may be used to increase the frequency with which responses are required. In these cases, several outs may be given to each player.

NOTES:  1. The instructor may adjust the rhythm to keep the group properly challenged.
   2. The instructor can also decide whether the blank word must be syntactically correct in the sentence or not. (I usually play this game with the rule that any word is acceptable, as long as it is a real word and has not already been used.)

COMMENTS: This is actually an old Victorian parlor game, and possibly dates back even earlier than that. It is useful in sharpening an ensemble's concentration, and getting them in touch with their associative powers. The great thing about this exercise is that it can only be done successfully if the player's mind is relaxed. It therefore forces them to relax and allow their associative powers to flow.

## Metaphor Description

PURPOSE: To associate aspects of one object in a description of something else.

DESCRIPTION: Each player is to hold in mind a visual image of an object, e.g., a rose, the sun, a horse. They are then to use the image of this object to draw descriptive language on a chosen subject, person, place, or thing. For example, with a rose, one might describe a woman as "she was soft and fragrant as she blossomed from youth, but she hid in her heart a painful sting for the unwary admirer."

NOTES:   1. These descriptions can be spoken or written, then shared with the rest of the group.
2. Players give their descriptions, then see if the group can guess their model image.

COMMENTS: This exercise leads actors to a better awareness of the associative process. The technique can also be very useful in developing detail for improv assumptions. It is also a simple and effective technique for being more colorful in one's descriptions.

INCORPORATION

*The mind loves wholeness.*
This final section of Freeing the Imagination demonstrates how spontaneity and association are combined for a creation with *structure*. The following exercises show how the free and arbitrary processes explored thus far may be guided to achieve an improviser's deliberate intent. (See Chapter Eleven of *The Art of Play*.)

Once actors have a command of free association, they may move into incorporation exercises. They may be somewhat relieved at this point that they can finally "make sense." Reincorporate the concepts of trust, spontaneity, and free association in these sessions. Actors must see how these components merge into the *creative thought process*. They must be able to recall this process at will; *then* they are ready to tackle the "rules of improv," and apply them to the improvised scene. This takes place in the next phase.

## Unrelated Phrases

PURPOSE: To incorporate disparate images into a whole narrative.

DESCRIPTION: The full group breaks up into groups of three. Player One and Player Two sit on the floor facing each other while Player Three sits to the side. (P3 has a watch with a second hand.) P1 thinks of three unrelated phrases, such as: "the dog has fleas," "the mountains rolled like thunder," and "Peewee hit a home run." (P1 must be careful not to choose associated phrases such as "Mom returned from the grocery store," and "We had lasagna for dinner.") Once P1 has chosen the phrases, he or she then recites them one at a time to P2, then repeats them once. P3 waits for P2 to speak, then begins timing him or her for one minute. In that time, P2 must create a narrative that incorporates all three unrelated phrases. The example above might be incorporated like this: "The Himalayan Little League's last game was about to be called due to the impending storm. The Dogs had never won the series. Peewee stood at the plate as the crowd jeered, 'the Dog has fleas!' The mountains rolled like thunder as the referee called for the last pitch. He swung with all his might, and when it was over, Peewee hit a home run, to win the game." The exercise continues by players rotating roles until each has done all three roles. Players may then make the exercise more challenging by adding additional unrelated phrases: four, then five, etc.

NOTES: 1. P2 must concentrate fully on memorizing the phrases as they are recited, and incorporate them as close to word for word as possible.
2. P2 cannot create a long, rambling narrative and simply drop the phrases in as he/she goes along. It is not enough to string together the phrases, the ideas and images themselves must be *incorporated* into a single context or situation.

COMMENTS: This is an excellent exercise for honing incorporation skills. Players will find that if they relax and allow their minds to free-associate with each phrase given, they will have ample choices with which to incorporate the ideas into one. Also, if they create a visual image of the phrase, they will remember it better. With practice, players should be able to incorporate five or more unrelated phrases within the time allotted.

## Half-wit

PURPOSE: To experience incorporation, and to practice relinquishing preconceived ideas.

DESCRIPTION: A full group breaks up into smaller groups of at least three players. Players One and Two stand together hip to hip facing the other player(s), with arms around each other's shoulders. P1 and P2 are the *half-wit*. P3 gives the half-wit a topic of conversation. The half-wit discourses on that topic by each player speaking one word at a time, alternating the words between them. The half-wit's discourse should last two or three minutes. P1 and P2 conclude the discourse themselves, by finally arriving at the words "the . . . end."

NOTES:  1. P1 and P2 speak as one person to the group, not to each other.
2. The object is to make the half-wit's discourse smooth and conversational, as though only one person were speaking. The only criterion is that the narrative make syntactical sense.
3. Players should use inflection to telegraph additional meaning to their words, and to create an *attitude* for their half-wit.
4. Once the half-wit begins speaking, it continues without player comment, until the words "the end" are spoken.

COMMENTS: The beauty of this exercise is that with each word a player must relinquish an entire thought. For instance, if P1 began with the word "my" (thinking, "My brother-in-law is a lawyer"), and P2 responded with "goodness" (as in "My goodness, you look fit"), P1 must respond to the words "my / goodness," discard his or her previous thought, and immediately form a new thought, such as "my / goodness, / Bill . . ." and so on.

## Half-wit—Group Variation

PURPOSE: To experience incorporation, and to practice relinquishing preconceived ideas as a group.

DESCRIPTION: Two groups of three to six players face each
other. Each group stands tightly together with arms around each
other's shoulders making a *single half* of the half-wit. A topic is
given, and the starting group forms a single collective word; first
one group says a word, then the other, and so on, alternating
one word at a time.

NOTES:  1. Groups should not have leaders who initiate words,
           but all in the group should *follow* each other. (Words
           will come slowly and often start with a single elon-
           gated sound, until the collective word is discovered,
           e.g., "*Mmyyy / dddooogg / hhhaaasss / fffllleeeaass!*")
        2. If the group members have difficulty not initiating,
           ask them to close their eyes.

COMMENTS: This exercise can lead to some surprising results if
the group is well attuned to each other. Expect the narrative to
develop slowly. Most words will end in an upward inflection.
Encourage the group to try to add a more natural inflection to
their words.

## Half-wit—Scene Variation

PURPOSE: To experience Half-wit within the context of a scene.

DESCRIPTION: Four players create two half-wits who will play
characters in a scene. Variables for the scene are chosen such
as character relationship and location. The scene begins with
each half-wit delivering one line of dialogue at a time.

NOTES: Half-wits should remain connected at the hip with outer
hands free. They are to move about, and perform actions as the
scene requires.

COMMENTS: This exercise adds a new level of incorporation in
that ideas now must be incorporated logically into the context of a
scene. Players now not only associate with words and inflections,
but also with the actions of the other half-wit in the scene. A fun

variation is to have the entire group play half-wit characters at a party. The instructor may call out different locations such as a party at the White House or a child's birthday party.

## Expert

PURPOSE: To spontaneously incorporate new ideas without showing any visible effort.

DESCRIPTION: An *expert* and an *interviewer* are chosen. The interviewer chooses from the group's suggestions a topic upon which the expert is an expert on. Unusual topics should be chosen, such as pet counselor, cloud sculptor, etc. The expert plays the world's foremost expert on this particular topic. The interviewer will engage the expert in a line of questioning designed to extract the most detail possible on the topic.

NOTES:  1. The expert must speak with utter confidence and authority at all times, and never seem hesitant or at a loss for an answer.
   2. The interviewer's job is to challenge the expert to provide specific details asking *what, when, where, how*. The interviewer must not be drawn into the absurdity of the topic, but must always ground his or her questions in logic and common sense.

COMMENTS: The essence of this exercise is mastering the ability to mask one's own thought process. A true expert always has the answers, and speaks in a matter-of-fact, self-assured manner. I have found it helpful to set up this exercise by having one player be an expert on a topic he or she is *truly* an expert on, his or her family for instance. I then have the group describe the expert's responses, noticing the physical details, swiftness in responding, attitude, confidence, etc. This gives them a model for how they must come off in the exercise.

## Reverend Whittaker's Alternative

PURPOSE: To see how a random incorporation of ideas can produce a result with continuity.

DESCRIPTION: A group of eight players is equipped with a pile of eight sheets of blank paper. The instructor determines the type of narrative to be created, e.g., romance, adventure, mystery. Names are chosen by the group for a *hero, heroine,* and *villain.* Each player writes a paragraph or so on each of the eight narrative parts below. After writing part one, the players place that sheet on the bottom of their pile of blank sheets, pass the entire pile to the player on their left, and accept a new pile from the player on their right. They then write part two, and repeat for all parts. The jumbled stories are then read aloud. The eight narrative parts are as follows:

1. The background and setting in which the hero is found.
2. The description of the hero.
3. His purpose in undertaking a quest, his destination, and what he expects to find there.
4. His enthralling journey through hostile regions. His discovery of the heroine, her looks, and the nature of her distress.
5. A description of the villain and his bestial practices.
6. The hero's bold exploits in rescuing the heroine from the villain. The fate of the foiled villain.
7. The triumphal return of the hero and heroine. The nature of the new relationship between hero and heroine.
8. The moral of the story.

NOTES: 1. Players should use colorful, descriptive language in their writing. Each player should be writing their own consistent story, even though they write each section on a different pile of paper.
2. The gender of the hero, heroine, and villain may be changed for added interest, but must remain consistent for all stories.

COMMENTS: This old parlor game is a good introductory exercise for incorporation. It is a fun way to prove to the group that incorporation need not be so difficult. This exercise is best done without the players realizing that their stories will be read as a jumble. This also works well as a period language or vocabulary exercise.

# Choices Phase 4

This phase of rehearsal entails taking the ideas laid out thus far, arriving at some inspired choices for character elements, then developing the character physically (the character's semblance). At the same time, the morning improv workshop should move into scene work skills, to prepare for improvising in character during the next phase.

## Development of Character Choices

Here the director has the often perilous task of guiding the actors through the process of making the choices that define character. Drawing upon the Freeing the Imagination workshop, try to keep them free and playful in their searching. Encourage them to apply their newfound spontaneity on creating without judgment or critical thinking. Remind them to trust their imaginations.

The overwhelming tendency will be for the actors to judge every idea harshly because of their desire to find the "best" ideas for their character. If you cannot inspire them to relax and let the ideas come to them without instant doubt, then at least you can force them to make *many* choices that they can later scrutinize. Force them to make multiple choices for every character element, regardless of how much they, or you, like this or that idea. Your battle cry should be *"Always create from a position of choice!"*

If they find an idea they are not sure they like, have them write it down before searching for a better one; it may later turn out to be better than they first thought. If they find the *perfect* idea, have them write it out, then find another perfect idea, then another. Ideas have no feelings. You do not insult them by turning your attention to another. In the end, you will return to the very best idea.

The Elements Discussion exercise lists some common pitfalls in choosing character elements. Watch this early decision stage carefully; it is best to correct weak choices *before* the actor becomes too attached to them. Guard against actors playing out personal scenarios in their character. Yes, the choices often are extensions of the actor's personality, but it is unwise to allow them to "work out their issues" through the character. Many will tend to do this without any conscious knowledge of it. If this is the case, don't bother to point it out; just steer them away from it.

It sometimes happens that two actors come up with the same choice for Passion or Foible. Choices for Passion are more often duplicated, since this is a broad choice to begin with. Duplicate choices are not necessarily bad. If the two characters have different occupations or themes, the question becomes how these similar choices will be executed. If the *treatment* of a choice is different, its effect in performance will be different. After all, many people share the same passions, but this doesn't make them duplicate personalities.

A choice is only as good as the interaction it engenders. Actors unacquainted with interactive performance will often arrive at very dramatic and interesting choices that simply won't play in performance. A common refrain will be "Yes, but how would you play that in performance, and how will you involve the guest?"

Another important thing to remember at the outset of developing a character is that the actor must never build a character that depends on other characters to be complete. Codependence doesn't work on the interactive stage. All character elements should be self-contained and evident.

## Machine Characterization

PURPOSE: To explore developing character through physical elements.

DESCRIPTION: The instructor assigns machines to each player in the group. These may be ordinary, everyday machines such as a vacuum cleaner or lawn mower, and should involve some sort of motion. Each player must use the *rhythm, motion,* and *personality* of the machine as the impetus for a characterization. They pair up, each with their own machine, explore the physicality and rhythm of the machine, then transform it into a person. Both characters then interact in a scene.

NOTES:  1. Actors are not to merely imitate these machines but to create a complete and believable person.
2. Actors are to ask themselves what feelings, mental impressions, and emotional levels are conjured by that machine. Then, incorporate those into their characterization.

COMMENTS: This exercise is a good primer for the actor's physicalization of character elements. Of particular importance here is finding the machine's rhythm and incorporating it into the character.

## Elements Discussion—Passion, Foible, Needs

PURPOSE: To examine character elements for poor or inconsistent choices prior to physicalization work.

DESCRIPTION: This exercise is simply a roundtable discussion where each actor presents their initial choices for characterization. It is a time where the instructor can assist the actor in filling in the gaps left by weak or missing choices and bring the ensemble up to date on that particular actor's work. Among the pitfalls the instructor should be scouting for are (a) choices too internal to be read by the audience; (b) negative choices that will make the character appear unapproachable; (c) choices that seem too fanciful or improbable to be believable; (d) historically inaccurate choices; (e) choices that don't work well together or seem to contradict one another; (f) choices that won't make the occupation evident or explore the theme of the character; and (g) choices that won't lead the actor to his or her primary activities or primary needs.

NOTES:  1. The instructor should be extremely careful not to be discouraging in this exercise. The discussion should remain within the context of *tipping the actors off to potential problems* and *requiring them to develop their ideas further.*

2. Many heads are better than one. I often encourage the ensemble to suggest new ideas when the actor has reached an impasse.

COMMENTS: This "character doctor" workshop can be time-consuming, but it is also very important. The best time to correct weak choices is *before* the actor begins using them. Most actors will hungrily accept this kind of input, and if a proper temenos is created, they will gladly look to their fellow ensemble members for supportive ideas. This exercise can be repeated later in the process, if necessary.

## Group Brainstorm on Others' Choices

PURPOSE: To enhance character choice possibilities by using the imagination of fellow ensemble members.

DESCRIPTION: This exercise is simply a brainstorming session where actors gather in small groups to brainstorm possible choices for each other's characters. It begins by one actor explaining where he or she is in thinking about character. A discussion ensues on character elements the group feels would be interesting to play, yielding as many choices as possible. No input is provided by the actor whose character is being discussed. The actor's job is only to record each and every possibility for later scrutiny.

NOTES:  1. Make sure the group does not fall into a discussion over which choices are *better*. They are only to encourage any and every choice that seems interesting.
2. Remind each player not to let their group's excitement over particular choices color their decision. They alone are masters of their character's fate.

COMMENTS: Actors can glean a great deal of information and support through this exercise. It will not only give them ideas to consider, but will help establish a rapport of mutual support among the ensemble.

## Characters at Home Alone

PURPOSE: To help actors experience the private life of their characters.

DESCRIPTION: Each character enters the space alone, and performs a short scene. This scene always takes place in the "home" of the character. Upon entering they first define the space for us, in as accurate and detailed a manner as possible. (They are to reveal the size and design of their abode, as well as the items within it that reflect the character's personality.) The brief action of the scene is centered upon the question, "*What does the character do at home alone, when no one else is watching?*" (Having sex is not included.)

NOTES: 1. These scenes are nonverbal, unless the character decides to talk to him- or herself.
2. Coach lines include *Give us the visual! Move about the space! Define it physically for us!*
3. Stress that the goal of these scenes is not to be comic, but to make the character "human," and expose its innermost self.

COMMENTS: These scenes give the actors yet another psychological base for relating to their characters, and help their fellow ensemble members to understand their true nature.

## *Development of Semblance*

*Semblance* is the sum of the character's look, personality, vocal quality, and use of language. The process of creating the character's semblance is one of *personifying* the character elements and essential qualities previously discussed.

Once actors have made enough choices, they can zero in on the ones that seem most playable and that excite their imaginations. Have them use these choices in the following series of exercises, and cultivate a semblance. (See Chapter Eight of *The Art of Play.*)

Making the conceptual choices physical will either galvanize those concepts into a whole character or will let the actor (or director) know that other choices need to be explored. Know that this is all right; trial and error is part of the creative process and has no bearing on the quality of one's work.

In helping actors find the physicality and voice of the character, you may find yourself balancing the *extraordinary* with the *exaggerated*. (You want extraordinary, not exaggerated.) The character should stand out in a crowd and be recognizable, but should always remain *believable*.

Also watch for physicality or voices that may not be sustainable for the length of performance. The consequence is a physicality or vocal quality that will be dropped during performance, or an actor with strained muscles and no voice.

PHYSICALITY

The process of physicalizing the character is *the search for the physical details that inform and convince the audience of who the character is*. These physical details include the way that a character stands, walks, and moves; their rhythms, mannerisms, and idiosyncratic gestures. All of these things combine to make the character physically *evident*.

## Physicality Parade

PURPOSE: To show the actor unknown aspects of their personal physicality, so that they may deliberately separate them from the character's physicality.

DESCRIPTION: Six or eight actors stand in a large circle facing inward. One actor is asked to enter the circle and begin walking around the inside periphery. The actor is told to do nothing but walk in a normal everyday manner, and with as little self-conscious affectation as possible. Meanwhile, actors in the circle are asked to examine the walker's physicality carefully. After two or three revolutions, an actor from the circle, Imitator One, is asked to fall in behind the walker, and imitate as precisely as they can the walker's physicality, magnifying it only slightly. This actor should then choose and make evident certain elements of the walker's physicality that attract the observer's attention. After several more revolutions I ask another actor to join in behind the first imitator. Imitator Two must then imitate the physicality of Imitator One (not the original walker). Here again, certain key elements will be magnified by Imitator Two. The process continues until there are five or six imitators walking in a line, each more magnified and heightened than the previous, with the last imitator absurdly broad, but very reminiscent of the original walker. The walker then steps out and inspects the parade, and their own magnified mannerisms.

NOTES:  1. The original walker must walk as if unaware that anyone was watching.
2. Imitators notice the rhythms used to walk, how the body sways, the gait, how the head is held, shoulders, hips, what their attitude seems to be, etc. Remind them that the idea is not to exaggerate, but to magnify.

COMMENTS: This exercise is mortifying, but in a fun way, and really shows the actors what aspects of their own physicality they must be careful to eliminate from their characterization. Often there are distinctive aspects the actor may not have realized they had.

## Magnify Presence

PURPOSE: To widen the actor's sphere of energy and create a larger personal presence.

DESCRIPTION: Actors stand in a relaxed, neutral position. After a few deep breaths they are asked to become aware of their personal space and are led through the following visualization. "Place your focus on the volume of air around your whole body, from six inches away to the surface of your skin. Imagine that that space around you is a field of your most potent, personal energy, or presence. Anything entering that field becomes a part of you, and you a part of it. Now inhale deeply, and as you do, imagine that field expanding one foot outward from your body in all directions. Do this with an attitude of welcoming and calm. As you exhale, the field retains its new size, but its potency remains undiminished from the inner field. It is as though your energy field has doubled in size without losing any energy. Take a moment to imagine this field around you and feel *larger*. Now continue to expand this sense of self by once again inhaling deeply and visualizing your energy field widening, this time by two feet. With each breath, imagine your field widening twice the amount of the previous breath (i.e., two feet, four feet, eight feet, sixteen feet, thirty-two feet, sixty-four feet, etc.). Breathe and widen your space until it fills the room, then extends beyond the room, so that the room is contained within your own personal energy field. Maintaining that image, begin to move about the room, feeling that everything in it and around it is a part of you. You have now magnified your presence."

NOTES: 1. This exercise should not represent to the actor an *output of energy*, but rather a *shift of perception*. They simply feel their sense of self widening, and it becomes so.
2. They should perceive everything within their widening field with a sense of warmth and acceptance, even joy and fulfillment.
3. Changes in their physical appearance should be minor, but there should be a noticeable change in presence. Actors should feel this sphere of energy emanate from a center placed not in their head, but in their heart.

COMMENTS: Actors who disapprove of themselves may find this exercise difficult or uncomfortable. Nonetheless, it is only a shift in perception and takes only concentration to achieve. Actors successful in this will have a more impressive aura about them and will noticeably *twinkle*. This, I believe, is what they call "star quality."

I use the next series of exercises (from Body Centers to Mill and Seethe Tasks) to begin the physicalization process, and I do them as a continuous string that can last over an hour and a half. This workshop has never failed to give actors a true feel for their character's physicality and vocal quality, or to uncover areas that need rethinking.

## Body Centers

PURPOSE: To find the character's "body center."

DESCRIPTION: This exercise is nonverbal. The company forms a large circle, as large as the rehearsal space can accommodate. All begin to walk in a clockwise direction in their normal walk while the exercise is explained. They are asked to become aware of their walk (rhythms, gait, etc.). Then they are asked to imagine a string entering the crown of their head, extending down through their spinal column, and attached to their body's center of gravity. They are *hanging* from this string as if they were a puppet dangling from its head string. Everything else is relaxed and hanging loosely from the string, which bears them up and slightly forward; this gives them a neutral walk (their *neutral body center*). The body center is their body's *dynamic center of gravity and energy*. It is where their movement comes from. They now move their body center to their breastbone by imagining that the string is now connected to their sternum and is pulling them upward and forward from that point. Their new body center informs their whole physicality in a natural and relaxed way. Immediately their physicality changes and their movement takes on a whole different tone. It is as though each different body center has its own accompanying attitude. For instance, a body center attached to the breastbone and angled upward and forward will tend to make most people feel pride. A body center on the end of the chin may be read as sternness, at the end of the nose an attitude of snobbery is suggested, and so on. Various centers are called out to them, and they are asked to examine how these changes make them feel. They then experiment on their own. Afterward, they are asked to consider their characters and begin exploring possibilities for their character's body center.

NOTES:  1. If actors get dizzy from walking so long in a circle, reverse directions or allow them to mill and seethe about the space.
2. Coach them regularly to relax and let the body follow the center. As they experiment, encourage them to try different vectors (directions) for each center, and notice its effect.
3. Allow more than one body center, but no more than two. They may combine in some rhythmical pattern, such as an undulating set of shoulders.

COMMENTS: Every character's physicality can be defined by a body center. The idea is very helpful because it would be impossible for an actor to mentally juggle all the various details of physicality while engaged in a spontaneously improvised performance. Generally what happens is that the physicality wears off; little by little the nuances of those choices are forgotten by the actor while improvising. The beauty of body centers is that we are embodying the whole of the character's movement "package" into a single idea. This makes it far easier to sustain in performance. As long as the actors allow the center to inform the rest of their body, a very natural and consistent physicality will result.

## Mill & Seethe Greeting

PURPOSE: To experience interrelating new characterizations nonverbally.

DESCRIPTION: This nonverbal exercise takes place in character, using body centers. Characters are asked to mill about the space. When they pass another character (the next one to catch their eye), they are to make eye contact, smile, and move on. Other subtle ways of engaging another human being are then added, as they continue to mill and seethe. They may be asked to stop, make eye contact, bow, shake hands, tip their hat, etc. Each greeting is positive in tone and is accompanied by direct eye contact.

COMMENTS: This helps them to warm into interrelating with another character, without the demands of scene work that may break their concentration on physicality.

## Mill & Seethe Gifts

PURPOSE: To experience a new characterization in a nonverbal, outward expression of giving.

DESCRIPTION: This nonverbal exercise is done following the Mill & Seethe Greeting exercise. It is performed in character, using body centers. Actors mill and seethe about the space, and are asked to imagine that they carry a possession small enough to easily hold in their hands. This item is of great sentimental value or importance to them. As they meet another character, they present this item to them. The receiving character shows appreciation (nonverbally), takes the gift, and then presents their own gift to the giver. The giver receives it in like manner, then both continue milling and repeat the same process with each character they meet. Gifts are given in such a way that it is reasonably clear what the object is that is being given, without getting into a game of charades. Gifts should be given excitedly, and received with great appreciation and thanks, for precious things are being transferred.

NOTES: 1. Explain that characters are created to be *given away* to the guest. The giving of their gift is analogous to the giving of their performance.
2. Actors are to make eye contact, and focus on the joy of giving something of value.
3. Exchanges should not build into lengthy scenes; keep it moving.

COMMENTS: This always creates the proper mood for giving a character performance. For the sake of interest, I sometimes finish this with each person describing what gifts they are left with, to see if anyone recognizes their original object.

## Mill & Seethe Emotions

PURPOSE: To explore the emotional levels of the character.

DESCRIPTION: This exercise should be done after Mill & Seethe Gifts. It is performed in character, using body centers. Characters mill and seethe about the space. As they do, emotions are called out to the group that they are then to exhibit as they feel the character would. They may do this physically, verbally, or nonverbally, but they are not to interact with another character. Characters may speak to an imaginary person, but not to each other. Twenty or thirty different emotions are called out with a varying intensity from one to the next.

NOTES: When calling out emotions, try escalating them before moving to the next, e.g., *"anger . . . really angry . . . absolutely raving!"* This forces actors to commit to the emotion and use their vocal quality and physicality in different ways.

COMMENTS: This exercise can be of use any time the cast needs to take the characterizations further, or to revitalize them.

## Mill & Seethe Tasks

PURPOSE: To experience the transaction of a character need.

DESCRIPTION: This exercise should follow the Mill & Seethe Emotions exercise. It is done in character using body centers. Actors mill and seethe about the space. This exercise proceeds exactly as the Mill & Seethe Gifts exercise, except instead of gifts, characters exchange tasks. The characters may speak during this exercise. Each character is given a moment to come up with a specific task, a here and now activity, that they need another human being to perform for them (an *active choice*). The task should be drawn from the character's primary activities or primary needs. First one has its task accomplished, then the other; then they move on to the next character.

NOTES:  1. Coach actors to keep the dialogue brief, and not to launch into scene work.
           2. Tasks must be performed as asked, without any hesitation or attitude of any kind. It is assumed by both characters that the task is one that will be joyfully performed. Tasks should never be intentionally abusive or difficult.

COMMENTS: This exercise, when performed in series with those listed previously, finally gives the actor a chance to interact with another character. The building of anticipation is useful. The actor is weaned into interacting after having time to feel somewhat comfortable with the character. This prevents them from falling into old habits, having their play be inhibited by self-judgment, or playing for the benefit of their fellow ensemble members.

## Physicalize Passion, Foible, Needs

PURPOSE: To explore physicalizing character elements.

DESCRIPTION: The group members mill and seethe around the space and find their characters' body center. The instructor then calls out character elements, one at a time. Actors fill their awareness with that one aspect of character and search for ways of showing it physically. The instructor calls out, "Passion," "Foible," "Needs," and "Virtue," providing several minutes for each one to be explored. Actors are then given a few moments to merge all these elements into one physicality. After, the group is brought together again, and new discoveries are shared.

NOTES: As each element is called out, coach actors to *Explore only the essence of the element called, in isolation from the others! Relax and play! Use your bodies to explore, not your minds! Examine posture, rhythm, gesture, and idiosyncrasy! Reveal your elements!*

COMMENTS: This exercise provides creative time to work out the nuances of physicality. Don't let the actor get bogged down in trying to create a physical road map to each character element. Some choices will be subtle.

## Character Song/Rhythm

PURPOSE: To clarify a character's rhythm, and to create a hook for connecting to it.

DESCRIPTION: Actors mill and seethe about the room in character. As they move, they exaggerate their physicality until a clear rhythmic pattern emerges. They continue to heighten and clarify that rhythmic pattern and create a "song" utilizing it. This song may be sung with words or with any collection of sounds, or hummed, but it must be *distinct and repeatable*. When it is sung, it should remind the actor of the character's rhythms. This they may then use as a hook for finding that rhythm whenever they need to.

NOTES: It is best if the song is one that would not seem out of context in performance.

COMMENTS: Actors may use their character's song to get into character before the performance begins, and may use it to reconnect to the character during performance if they feel their physicality or their commitment to their character is waning.

## Character Parade

PURPOSE: To view characterizations.

DESCRIPTION: This exercise is conducted as a dress parade would be for costumes. Each character in turn enters the space exhibiting their character's physicality, mannerisms, and body rhythms. Upon reaching the center of the performance space, they introduce themselves and speak on a topic, or in such a way that reveals their occupation, foible, and needs. Once those elements are established, they motivate an exit, and remain in character until completely out of the performance space.

COMMENTS: I use this exercise both early in the development

process to help focus the characters and late in the process to confirm for everyone what each has created.

Ideally, the vocal quality of the character comes from the physicality. Use the Voice from Body exercise to achieve a vocal quality that fits the body and movement of the character.

Beyond a voice that reveals character, the chief concern should be diction and projection. A voice is nothing if not heard in performance. Interactive environments can offer formidable vocal challenges. Be certain you use open and well-supported sound.

Often, actors looking for a unique character voice will immediately tighten their throat and rasp out an interesting but vocally destructive sound. Placement is best in the mask of the face, not in the throat or chest. (Be prepared, however, to adjust some annoyingly nasal tones.) Contrary to what might be believed, there is a great deal of characterization to be had in a strong head voice. Have them experiment with inflection and attitude. The cadence and music of the voice can create character just as well as its tone.

## Voice from Body

PURPOSE: To elicit a natural vocal quality from the character's physicality.

DESCRIPTION: After settling on a body center for the character, actors choose a phrase they think their character might say: an axiom or oath, indicative of that character's outlook. Then while moving in character, they are asked to say that oath aloud and *without any preconceptions of vocal quality*. They are to let their character's voice *come from their physicality*. If the actors can disconnect their mental processes from this, their bodies will do the work for them, and an open and relaxed character voice will emerge naturally. They practice this, then experiment with other oaths.

COMMENTS: This more organic approach to vocal quality will prevent them from coming up with a character voice that seems contrived, that does not seem to match the character's movement.

# Optimum Voice

PURPOSE: To practice adjusting vocal projection to the character's proper sphere of influence.

DESCRIPTION: In this exercise the actor interrelates two vocal
variables. One is the vocal level, i.e., intimate—speaking quietly
to one person; conversational—speaking moderately to one or
several people; or projected—calling out to one or more people.
Two is their *projection*, i.e. the sphere of influence around the
actor, whose radius is the distance between them and the most
distant guest who should be able to hear them—their *volume*.
Player One begins with an intimate vocal level spoken at a natural projection, then P1 extends to a greater projection, then
greater, and greater still. They do this while maintaining the
same vocal level. They repeat this for the conversational level,
and then a projected level. The exercise continues until each
player has gone. The full group may then experiment at will,
within the performance space.

NOTES:  1. The aim is to acquaint the actor with being deliberate in his or her vocal projection. To be able to fill
the space with *not more* but *not less* volume than
what is required, and to do this while preserving the
intended vocal level.
2. If rehearsal space allows, have players move to the
extremity of the sphere of influence as it is changed,
then judge whether the volume and vocal level is
appropriate.

COMMENTS: There is a threefold benefit to learning *optimum
voice*: first, to learn to project so that the character will be over-
heard by guests; second, to preserve the actor's voice by learning
not to use more projection than is required for the circumstance;
and third, to learn to preserve the level of intimacy through
increased projection, so that the entire performance environment
does not sound like a bunch of screeching characters.

### COSTUME, PROPS, AND ACCESSORIES

Cultivate and encourage ideas at this point, but not until the character is more firmly developed should production time be spent
on specific changes to the costume design and accessories, or the

creation of hand props. Although these are part of the character's semblance, it is too early for actors to confirm these choices; have them merely make note of ideas as they come up. By the end of the next phase, however, actors should finalize these items.

## Improv Scene Work

Present the tenets of good scene work in a way that doesn't let critical thinking and judgment reenter the picture, after you so carefully erased it in the Freeing the Imagination workshop. Scene work takes actors the next step, beyond personal spontaneity. The focus is on taking the process covered thus far for the individual player and applying it to the collective process of spontaneity *among* players. This is where players are called upon to "share their toys." Establish good habits in making and accepting assumptions, listening, focus, and aspiring to the goals of trust, support, and cooperation. Pay particular attention to the problems of selectivity and playing for control, such as steamrolling and scriptwriting. These are killers of good scene work. (See Chapter Twelve of *The Art of Play*.)

Accomplish this by drawing from the basics of play. If you can eradicate the poisons of judgment and comparison here, and keep the spirit of the work playful, joyous, and supportive, you will do more for the success of the ensemble than at any other time in the rehearsal process.

It is part of our natures to desire not only to excel, but, unfortunately, to *excel without ever having failed*. As the complexities of scene work are brought together, actors will invariably admonish themselves for their poor attempts. It is imperative that, here, the actor be made to understand that in order to excel, one must fail, and that in this context *it is all right to fail*. Most assuredly, they will regard this as mere lip service intended to make them feel better, until the instructor makes them see that *how we fail is at least as important as how we succeed*. There is nothing wrong with failure! Both have value in learning something new; indeed, nothing of value is ever learned without a measure of error. Yet we desperately seek to negate the importance of error in our learning.

The ensemble must be a place where failure is accepted—not intended certainly, but accepted. Yes, perhaps even enjoyed. Imagine for a moment the freedom this brings to creativity. Instead of denying and feeling ashamed of our failed attempts, we embrace them and explore them for insight, thus we excel greater and faster. Our success *confirms* knowledge, but our failure *exposes* it. As the actor wades through the inevitable mediocrity of learning improv scene work, or applying it to a new ensemble, I strongly reinforce every success I see, but I also relate positively to their mistakes. I am often heard saying things like "Thank you for that mistake, now we can all take a look at it." "Sure it sucked, but you took the risk, so good for you! Now what did you learn?" "Let's agree that its okay to suck, that's what rehearsal is for!" An ensemble that treats failure as just another tool for success ignites a creative force that is nearly miraculous!

Begin with the Think Tank exercise, and start two-player scenes with the "Yes, and . . ." Scene exercise. Do not improvise in character yet; keep this improv abstract in order to concentrate fully on the technique. Continue two-player scene work as you add exercises that build the techniques below. (Multiple-player scenes may begin when you cover second support.) This section gives ample exercises to cover these areas:

- Positive assumption technique
- The skill of listening
- Giving and taking focus in a scene (when to and when not to)
- Breaking the habit of asking questions (interrogatives)
- Secondary support of a scene
- Dominance transactions

POSITIVE ASSUMPTION EXERCISES

## Think Tank

PURPOSE: To affirm and build upon another player's ideas.

DESCRIPTION: The full group is broken into groups of four to six players, who sit in a circle facing inward. All are deemed to be the world's foremost experts in their field. Every word from their mouths is seen as a pearl of wisdom and genius. The group's task is to create an invention: a physical object or machine that accomplishes a particular purpose or set of tasks. Player One, uninterrupted, describes one element of this invention. P1 may begin with "I believe our invention needs yellow balloon tires in order to move over rough terrain." When P1 is finished, other players express their approval and appreciation for P1's genius. P2 then describes an element, building upon the machine with "yellow balloon tires." Each player, in turn, adds to the invention until all players have spoken twice. The invention is named, and one person from the group is given the task of giving a presentation on their invention to the other groups.

NOTES: 1. Players must never interrupt the players speaking, even if it is in support of their idea. Once a player begins speaking, that player has the floor until he or she gives it up.
2. Players must never negate or minimize in any way the elements added to the invention by another player. It is important that all players join in the spirit of mutual awe and admiration.
3. Inventions should not be limited by practicality or the laws of physics. This is a "blue sky" phase of development, where anything is possible.

COMMENTS: The importance of this exercise lies in the mutual support of the players, the unquestioning acceptance of another player's ideas, and the cooperation required in incorporating all of the ideas into a whole. Each player will feel that they have made a substantial contribution to the whole. No one person is in control; all share responsibility equally. This exercise is directly analogous to good ensemble scene work.

## "Yes, and . . ." Scene

PURPOSE: To focus on accepting assumptions and using them to build new information.

DESCRIPTION: Two players begin a scene. Each time a player responds to dialogue, they must preface their response with the two words "Yes, and. . . ." For example:
Player One: "Boy it's hot in here."
Player Two: "Yes, and as fire chief you should have known better than to get yourself trapped in a burning building."
P1: "Yes, and since I am the only member of the fire department, it doesn't look like we'll be getting any help soon."
The instructor stops the scene before the conflict is resolved, and asks the actors to replay the scene from the beginning, as closely as possible to the original, but without the words "yes, and." When players reach the point at which the scene was stopped, they continue on to resolve the conflict and conclude the scene.

NOTES: 1. Actors must follow the spirit of "yes, and," and not only affirm the previous assumption, but use that assumption as the basis for their next assumption.
2. When the scene is replayed, players may embellish the somewhat stilted dialogue of the initial scene, but must follow the original assumptions in their same order.

COMMENTS: The "yes, and" crutch will make dialogue seem halting and unnatural, but the ideas will be built more clearly. In replaying the scene, players are more comfortable, knowing where the scene is headed. The idea is that the feeling of mutual support and affirmation will carry over past the cutoff point, allowing the actors to experience a true positive assumption process.

## Niagara Falls

PURPOSE: To focus on accepting assumptions.

DESCRIPTION: Two players begin a scene. After a brief exchange, Player One becomes stricken by a word or phrase presented by Player Two in the scene, apparently loaded with personal meaning. This phrase sends P1 on a *brief* but *acute* emotional tirade of some sort, e.g., hatred, jealousy, confusion, or sadness. This tirade recounts the disastrous or meaningful experience that was triggered by the phrase, such as "Niagara Falls! My brother was killed at Niagara Falls. . . ." When P1 calms down, the dialogue continues until P2 is stricken with a similarly potent word or phrase spoken by P1. This process continues until the scene concludes or is cut by the instructor.

NOTES: 1. A *coherent* scene must still be maintained between the outbursts.
2. Players may toy with each other in the scene by deliberately offering possible "Niagara Falls phrases," creating a fun sense of suspense.

COMMENTS: This scene is about *overaccepting* assumptions. It should show actors just how far a simple piece of information can be made to go; how valuable one player's support of another player's assumption can be; and how powerful a strong emotional state can be in creating interest. It can be very helpful in creating a sense of mutual trust and support.

## Blocking Scene

PURPOSE: To experience the difficulties arising from one player blocking the invention of another.

DESCRIPTION: Two players begin a scene (variables for the scene may be chosen). Player One's objective is to *initiate new assumptions and to inspire the forward movement of the scene.* Player Two's objective is to *resist the invention of P1, by blocking or negating P1's assumptions.* P1 accepts and says *yes,* and P2 rejects and says *no.* When stopped by the instructor, P1 and P2 switch roles.

NOTES: 1. P1 must agree with P2's negations. For example:
        P1: "Hi, Mom, I'm home."
        P2: "I'm not your mother."
        P1: "Yes, that's right. I keep forgetting, my real mother died in a plane crash and you raised me since I was two."
    2. Observers should note how slowly the scene develops and how much effort is required of P1 without the partner's support.

COMMENTS: The purpose here is not to train actors to negate their partners, but to allow them to experience what negation feels like so that they can be more aware of it in their work.

## Interpreted Assumptions

PURPOSE: Focus on accepting the other player's interpretation of your assumption.

DESCRIPTION: The full group stands in a circle facing inward. Player One makes a vague or nonspecific physical assumption to Player Two, such as holding out an open hand and stamping a foot: anything nonverbal where the offerer's specific intent is indiscernible. The offer must be *interpreted* by P2 and an immediate response given. P1 must accept the altered response as readily as if his or her intended assumption had been understood, and must then make an additional affirming assumption showing acceptance of P2's ideas. P2 then makes a nonspecific assumption to P3, and so on around the circle. The instructor may then break them up into smaller groups or pairs to practice further.

NOTES: Players giving nonspecific assumptions should open themselves to the feeling of having their ideas interpreted without feeling *mis*interpreted.

COMMENTS: Interpreted assumptions is useful when actors have trouble relinquishing their ideas in a scene, or when they attempt to bend a scene toward their own preconceptions. They must see that the only *important* idea is the one *established* for the audience.

## Contact Assumption Scene

PURPOSE: To practice making physical assumptions.

DESCRIPTION: Two players begin a scene (variables may be chosen). For each assumption made (e.g., each line of dialogue), players must make some form of physical contact with their partner, e.g., shaking their hand, patting them on their back, or stepping on their foot. Each time a player speaks, a new form of physical contact must be made. This contact must also make sense for the assumption and the scene.

NOTES: Encourage players to create an emotional level to their assumptions and let the emotion inspire the physical contact.

COMMENTS: This exercise inspires more physical and emotional choices in scene work, and helps actors out of the common rut of being "talking heads."

## This Is You . . .

PURPOSE: To experience focusing on one's partner's character, not one's own.

DESCRIPTION: Two actors stand facing each other prepared to trade assumptions as gifts being given. Player One mimes pulling an *assumption* (about the size of a baseball) out of their head and offering it to their partner. As they hand it over, they speak the assumption. Player Two, receiving it, says, "Thank you," and places the imaginary *assumption ball* into their chest (heart). P1 and P2 continue trading assumptions that each player might receive from their partner, and each assumption begins with the words "This is you. . . ." For example:

P1: "This is you, my mother, calling me in for supper."
P2: "This is you asking if you can go out to the basketball game with your buddies after dinner."
P1: "This is you refusing until I finished my homework."
P2: "This is you sneaking out the bedroom window to see the game."

NOTES: 1. Assumptions are always accepted graciously as if a great gift had just been given.
2. Each actor is concerned only with their partner's action in the scene, not their own.

COMMENTS: This exercise places the actor's mental focus on their partner, and vice versa. It is the proper placement of focus for improv assumptions, and what is meant by "making your partner look good."

LISTENING EXERCISES

## Double Conversation

PURPOSE: To focus on listening by challenging the mind to listen and respond to two different sources of information simultaneously.

DESCRIPTION: Player One is seated, and Players Two and Three are seated to either side, facing P1 (one at each ear). P1's objective is to listen and respond *fully* to each of the simultaneous conversations. P2 and P3's objective is to *command 100 percent of P1's attention*, at all times. Each may say or do anything to attract and hold P1's total attention, *except any sort of physical contact*. After about two minutes of conversation, the instructor stops the exercise. P1 decides which of the two conversations held his or her attention the best, and roles are rotated so that P2 is in the middle with P1 and P3 to either side. The rotation continues until all players have been the listener.

NOTES: 1. Speakers should experiment with different topics and approaches to their conversation. An aggressive approach may not be the best.
2. The listener must always be fully present in both conversations. They may not choose to ignore either speaker.

3. Speakers must be careful not to get absorbed in the other conversation, or wait for the opposite speaker to finish speaking. Each second the listener is listening to the other speaker is a second counted against them.

COMMENTS: The focus of this exercise is on the listener who must stretch his or her listening and comprehension skills, although the speakers learn a bit about assertive behavior and what types of things hold the attention of an individual.

## Listening to Environment

PURPOSE: To focus on the auditory sense.

DESCRIPTION: Players are to lie on the ground or floor with their arms flat to their sides, relax, and breath deeply. They are then asked to clear their minds, and to focus their attention on every detail of what they hear. From the loudest to the faintest sounds, they are to peel back each layer, and isolate as many individual sounds as possible, right down to the blood flowing through their ears. After the exercise, players are asked to list the isolated sounds that they heard.

COMMENTS: This exercise can be particularly interesting when performed outdoors, but will work just as well indoors. Many people simply become used to not listening. Use of this exercise can open the mind's awareness of the auditory sense and reawaken the actors' ability to listen and focus their attention outside their own thoughts.

## Listening While Telling

PURPOSE: To focus on listening while the mind is actively engaged in speaking.

DESCRIPTION: **Part One:** Player One and Player Two sit facing each other. Player Three is the timer, and sits to the side with a stopwatch. Before the exercise begins, P3 acquires two topics, but does not mention them to P1 or P2. When ready to begin, P3 gives one topic to P1, then the other topic to P2, and immediately begins timing. P1 and P2 speak their topics to each other simultaneously, concentrating as they speak on listening to and retaining the other player's discourse. P3 stops the discourse at seven or eight seconds, and *without comment*, cues P1 to repeat back P2's discourse as close to word for word as possible. When P1 has finished, P3 cues P2, again without comment, and P2 recounts P1's discourse. The exercise is repeated, and roles are rotated.

**Part Two:** The exercise proceeds just as above, except that at seven seconds, instead of stopping the discourse, the timer says "change," and each player immediately begins discoursing on the other player's topic. The timekeeper then stops the scene at fourteen seconds; each player recounts as much as they can recall of the other player's discourse, in the same manner as before.

NOTES:   1. The key to success in this exercise lies in being as automatic as possible in discoursing on the topic, leaving as much mental room for listening as possible.
2. Only after both players have repeated back the discourse can players clarify or correct each other on their accuracy.

COMMENTS: Often in improvisation, an actor is called upon to be aware of what is happening in the scene at the same time as they are engaged in a spontaneous discourse. This exercise is a real mindbender, but it is an excellent tool for expanding an actor's concentration and awareness of what is going on around him or her during a scene.

Focus Exercises

## Pick Up an Object

PURPOSE: To learn to tune in to and support another player's physical intentions.

DESCRIPTION: Player One and Player Two enter the playing space from opposite directions. As they meet together in the center, they must pick up an invisible object and carry it out of the playing space. Players do not know beforehand what the object is; they must discover it together and pick it up without thought or hesitation. It should also be apparent to observers what type of object it is by the way the players handle it.

NOTES:  1. Both players should appear to be certain of the nature of the object, just as if it were actually there. As players arrive at the object, they must sense each other's physical intentions and make their movements as seamless as possible.

2. As soon as it is clear to both players what the object is, they carry the object out of the playing space.

COMMENTS: The sixth sense exhibited in this exercise can be quite surprising at times. The more open and receptive the players are to the other player's physical intentions, the easier their agreement on what the object will be.

## Absolute Focus

PURPOSE: To teach players to support a single, clear focus.

DESCRIPTION: Three to five players take positions within the playing space, either seated or standing. Each player must have all the other players in their field of view. A location is chosen where fairly static activity commonly takes place, such as a doctor's waiting room, ski lodge, or train station. Without any speaking or sound, players create a scene in which only one player may move at a time. Observers are to watch the scene and allow their eyes to be attracted by any movement that calls their attention, making note of each time a split focus occurs. For the purposes of this exercise, a *split focus* means anytime more than one player's movement occurs at the same time. After a few minutes, the instructor stops the scene, and the observers recount to the players the points at which a split focus occurred. The players then get to resume the scene, or begin a new scene to try to incur fewer split foci. After several tries, a new group of players is chosen, and the original players join the observation group.

NOTES:  1. In this exercise the focus must always be deliberately given or passed to another player. Any player trying to take the focus will almost certainly cause a split.

2. Players must learn to perform acts, like handing another player a glass of water, in such a way that only one player moves at any given time.

3. The players must never seem frozen; they must remain animate, but in a state of no motion. They

must plan to conclude their physical actions before passing the focus, in such a way that they are not left in an unnatural, frozenlike position.
4. Players must also be cautious of ending their motion facing away from the other players, thereby cutting themselves off from seeing who is moving.

COMMENTS: This exercise takes the matter of focus to the extreme. In normal scene work, simultaneous movement or speaking, to a reasonable degree, may not adversely affect the focus, so the rules of the Absolute Focus exercise do not necessarily apply to scene work. Actors' awareness of focus, however, should be as acute as that required in this exercise.

## Pass the Balloon

PURPOSE: To illustrate give and take in scene work, and repair lost trust and cooperation.

DESCRIPTION: **Part One**: Two players enter the performance space with a balloon, and pass the balloon between them by batting it back and forth. The instructor first asks them to bat the balloon using their hands only, then adds the knees, the head, then any part of the body they wish, as their awareness grows.

**Part Two**: Choose a *who*, *what*, and *where* for the scene. The two players agree that the balloon represents the *control and focus* of the scene. Whoever possesses the balloon, possesses the focus. As each player passes the focus, they bat the balloon to their partner. Their attention should be on the scene, not on the balloon. The balloon is never made part of the scene; it is only a metaphor for the control and focus in the scene. The player without the balloon may *never* speak or otherwise take focus until given the balloon. The balloon (control and focus) should pass freely and often between the players.

NOTES:  1. Allow the players time for the novelty of the balloon to wear off, then require them to direct their play not toward the balloon, but directly to each other.
2. (Part One) Coach players to *Make eye contact! Agree to play! Give and take! Share! Create together! Focus on each other, not the balloon! Communicate!*
3. (Part Two) Coach players to *Pass the balloon! Share*

*the focus! Don't hold the balloon! Add just a piece and give it away! Build together!*

COMMENTS: I have found this exercise extremely beneficial for new ensembles, and especially helpful to older ensembles where give and take may have been lost. The exchange of focus will *always* remain clear, both to the observers and, most important, to the players of the scene. This silly contrivance can quickly become a very powerful tool of insight for improvisers, even the most experienced ones. For ensembles that are in need of repair work in trust and cooperation, I ask them to demonstrate by using the balloon the various ways in which focus is abused by other members of the ensemble. I ask them to "show me with the balloon where they hurt you." Using the balloon as a metaphor, actors will relish showing how focus is hogged, dropped, stolen, etc. They air their frustrations in a safe and playful way and, in the process, learn a lot about their ensemble's trouble spots. After all trouble spots have been revealed, I ask each actor to consider how many times *they themselves* have made those mistakes. This places on their shoulders the responsibility for improving the ensemble, and can initiate some very positive discussion and changes.

## Scene Without Words

PURPOSE: To share focus without dialogue.

DESCRIPTION: Two players enter the playing space, and begin a scene. Variables may be given to the players, such as character relationship, and location. A cohesive and understandable scene must ensue. Players may communicate with each other through looks, gestures, and actions, but no words are to be spoken. Another version adds two observers chosen to create sound effects appropriate to the action depicted, as well as add sound effects of their own, which might further the scene.

NOTES:  1. Players in this scene are not to appear mute. They are not presenting a scene in which the characters *cannot* talk, but one where they just don't happen to speak. They must not give the observer cause to ask, "Why don't they just speak?"
  2. Players must respond to every sound effect, and incorporate it into the scene.

COMMENTS: This exercise can show actors that reams of information can be telegraphed to the audience without the use of words. It should reinforce the importance of physicality in the scene, as well as the benefits of focusing true attention on their partners.

## Party Scene

PURPOSE: To give and take focus within a group using movement and voice.

DESCRIPTION: Six pairs of players enter the performance space and behave as though attending a cocktail party. Each pair stays together, although pairs may speak to one another. Pairs are numbered as teams, and when the instructor calls out a team's number, that team must have the focus of the scene; that team takes the focus, as all other teams give focus. The instructor continues to call out teams until the whole group seems comfortable with the give and take of focus. The instructor then informs them that they must give and take focus on their own, and the ensuing scene should show only one dominant team at any given time.

NOTES: Teams may only take focus when it is either *given* to them or *made available*.

COMMENTS: There is a tendency for teams to steal focus from another in this exercise, since with six teams, players are likely to feel useless or impatient when they do not have the focus for a long time. This may cause them to jump the gun.

INTERROGATIVE EXERCISES

## Question Scenes

PURPOSE: To practice translating questions to statements.

DESCRIPTION: Two players perform a scene whose action typically requires one player to ask questions, such as, conducting an interview or interrogation, standing at an information counter, or getting lost in a foreign country. Player One takes the role of the would-be questioner. P1's objective is to fill their need in the scene without asking a question. P2's role is that of the character with the information or the ability to fill the need. P2's objective is to place P1 in the position of having to ask a question. The scene ends when the need is filled. Players then switch roles and begin a new scene.

NOTES: 1. P2 may be vague or block P1 only as far as it is reasonable and serves their purpose. For example:
P1: "I need to find out where you were on the night of the fifteenth."
P2: "I'm sure you do."
P1: "I would like you to tell me where you were on that night."
P2: "Somewhere in this city."
2. P1 may make assumptions and alter the context of the scene. They may not, however, answer their own questions.

COMMENTS: It is important to note that in improv we do not *need* to ask a question, because we may simply answer it for ourselves, and make that assumption. This exercise, however, deals only with the *translation* of a question into a statement, for the purpose of retraining our minds not to automatically ask a question when information is needed.

## No Questions for One Day

PURPOSE: To realize how questions can be rephrased into statements. To realize the frequency with which questions are asked.

DESCRIPTION: Players are requested, during a break, or perhaps until the next day's workshop, not to phrase a single interrogative statement (question). It may be wisest initially to perform this exercise over a break, then work up to an overnight homework exercise.

NOTES: Truly any question can be phrased as a statement, and fulfill the same needs. For instance, when asking directions to the restroom say, "Please give me directions to the restroom" instead of "Where's the restroom?"

COMMENTS: If one can make it through a day or even a lunch break without asking a question, then one may certainly make it through an improv scene without asking one. In improv, your partner doesn't know the answer any more than you do, so just answer it for yourself and create a statement, in the form of a strong informative assumption.

SECOND SUPPORT EXERCISES

## Second Support Conversation

PURPOSE: To focus on understanding a scene before entering for second support.

DESCRIPTION: The full group counts off into groups of five. Teams may play this game simultaneously. Players One and Two choose a topic secretly, and begin a conversation on that topic as the three other team members look on. P1 and P2 never mention the topic, and although they may not make false statements, they endeavor to mislead other players. When one of the observing players thinks they have guessed the topic, they enter the scene and make a supporting assumption. Original team members may challenge newcomers if they believe they have not guessed the topic correctly, by tapping them on the shoulder. When challenged, a newcomer must whisper into the ear of the challenger what the topic is. If it is incorrect, that player is sent back to observe with one "strike." The exercise is over when all observing players either are successfully in the scene, or have acquired three strikes, thereby striking out.

NOTES:   1. Be specific in choosing the topic. P1 and P2's objective is not to *win*, but to challenge the other players. If players are unable to make any reasonable guesses, they should make the topic more obvious.
2. The instructor may wish to make it more difficult for P1 and P2 by not allowing them to use the word "it" in place of the topic.
3. Coach players to *Take a chance! Make a guess! Enter with a strong assumption!*

COMMENTS: This exercise can show actors the value of hanging on the periphery of the scene before entering, and the danger of blundering in with new assumptions without knowing what the scene is about. It is also an opportunity for an actor to experience entering with a strong and specific assumption. I often tell them, "If you are going to make a mistake in improv, make it a big one." Improv is a risky business, and not for the timid or tentative. Although it is true that in this exercise the original topic is always maintained, it should be noted that in scene work, second support assumptions are never denied.

DOMINANCE TRANSACTION EXERCISES

## Dominance Postures

PURPOSE: To demonstrate how physicality and mannerisms reveal dominance.

DESCRIPTION: Each actor from the group, one by one, enters the space and displays a physicality (nonverbal) that reveals either a high or low dominance. The group analyzes the physicality for the details that invoke the intended status. The exercise is over when all players have provided a high- and low-status physicality.

NOTES: Physicality includes stance, posture, facial expression, intensity, and focus in movement.

COMMENTS: This is a very direct exercise for actors to understand the various ways that physicality can affect dominance. A variation of this exercise involves one player entering with an established dominance, and the other presenting a dominance (either higher or lower than the other player) as a response or reaction to the first player's dominance. This allows the group to explore the power of both high and low dominance.

## Master-Servant Scene

PURPOSE: To experience the interrelationships of high- and low-dominance characters.

DESCRIPTION: Two players enter the space and begin a scene (variables may be chosen or not). One player plays the master, the other the servant. A master-servant relationship may take many forms: a slave and master, a teacher and student, a cult leader and initiate. Each player plays the social dominance accordingly, with the master dominant and the servant "indominant." Players begin the scene by fully establishing the dominance of the master, then endeavor to change the dominance to the servant. They continue to transact dominance as much as possible.

NOTES: The social dominance of master and servant remains throughout the scene, although personal dominance changes.

COMMENTS: This exercise is merely practice in dominance transactions. It should be made clear to the players that the social station initiates the scene with a predetermined dominance pattern. As long as the social dominance is not compromised beyond what is acceptable to the audience, the personal dominance can change freely, adding interest to the scene.

## Ultimate Master Scene

PURPOSE: To explore a maximum dominance gap.

DESCRIPTION: Teams of five to seven players are chosen and enter the performance space. One player is chosen as ultimate master of the universe, the remaining players play the most lowly and insignificant creatures of the universe. Low creatures are the servants of the ultimate master. The low creatures' objective is to please the master and to stay alive. The ultimate master's objective is to be pleased by the low creatures. At the slightest hint of disapproval, dissatisfaction, impatience, or discomfort, the ultimate master is to snap his or her fingers at the low creature in question, whereupon that creature immediately dies and remains dead for the remainder of the scene. This scene is over when all low creatures have been killed.

NOTES:  1. The ultimate master must not show the slightest bit of mercy or remorse. The U.M. should no more hesitate to kill a low creature than they would to brush a piece of lint from their sleeve.
2. The low creatures may employ any means whatsoever in order to stay alive. (The last low creature living may be considered victorious in the exercise.)
3. Coaching: *Stay alive at any cost! Don't hesitate to kill! Live your part! Remember it's just make-believe!*

COMMENTS: Some actors will find either role in this exercise vaguely disturbing. These actors need to separate their personal perceptions of dominance with that of the characters they play. Players must learn to both command dominance and relinquish it.

## Pecking Order

PURPOSE: To experience various dominance relationships.

DESCRIPTION: The full group counts off into teams of three. One team member is chosen as *boss*, another as *middleman*, the third as *lackey*. The team lines up in order of dominance—boss, middleman, and then lackey—and remains in a line throughout the scene. A task is chosen for the scene, such as starting a car or raising an anchor. Each player relates only to the player adjacent to him. (The boss only with the middle man, the lackey only with the middleman, and the middleman with either.) Orders come down the line, problems come up the line. The scene is over when the boss can no longer give a command that will solve the lackey's problem. Repeat until each team member has played all three roles.

NOTES: The lackey and the boss are unaware of each other's existence. The middleman takes personal responsibility for all orders and problems. He must overcome his frustrations while speaking to the boss, but may take out his frustrations on the lackey.

COMMENTS: In this exercise the boss is always *dominant*, the lackey is always "*indominant*," and the middleman must be a *dominance transactor*.

## Accepting Insults

PURPOSE: To learn to accept indominance easily.

DESCRIPTION: **Part One:** Each player in the group creates a list of ten to fifteen insults. They may be as creative as they wish, as long as they are insulting. The full group then exchanges lists so that no player has his or her own list. The group pairs off. Partners alternate delivering insults to each other. Each time an insult is delivered, its recipient must display the full, unrestrained emotional impact of the insult, e.g., flustered embarrassment, exasperated outrage, stunned silence, or weeping.

Only after a player allows the insult to completely *slay them*, may they return an insult of their own.

**Part Two:** Two players face each other as before, armed with lists of insults not of their own choosing. One player gives five insults in a row. With each insult the recipient reacts as in Part One, but also shows whole-hearted agreement with the insult and provides circumstantial justification for it. Example:

Insulter: "You couldn't hit the broad side of a barn with a Mack truck."

Recipient: "Yes, you're right, I admit it! I once threw myself at the ground, and missed!"

NOTES:  1. Insulters should inflict their insults as though the recipient completely deserves it.
2. Recipients must totally commit themselves to accepting the insult. Their responses must never defend themselves or offer excuses.

COMMENTS: The purpose for the random lists is so that insults cannot be construed as a personal slight (consciously or unconsciously) by the insulter. As actors, players must always remain supportive and forgiving of one another. However, as characters, actors must be entirely comfortable with taking the fall.

# Development 5
# Phase

Once actors are comfortable with their character choices, and scene work is well in hand, move into advanced character development exercises and scene work in character, and begin narrative skills. During this phase, actors also develop the character's background and begin rehearsing character-dependent scenarios.

## Advanced Character Development

The actor must now plumb the depths of the character they have created. Good choices are important, but now the characters must be workshopped to give each actor an *experiential* connection to his or her character. They need ample opportunity to experience their physicality and character choices as a whole, and in relation to other characters.

In the Choices phase actors worked mostly in their heads. This ensured that individual characters worked interactively, and that the themes of the production were upheld. Now they will work together in groups of characters and explore the environment of the production. Allow them to begin discovering these relationships. They will not make them firm until the Performance phase, but let them explore them now freely. This section is all exercises, but it will be directly followed by using characters in scene work. Here they will get more in touch with how to establish character information and exhibit the six essential qualities of interactive characterization; explore using the character's primary needs to create action; and develop a sense of the character's values and attitudes.

Be open to the further development of character elements at this stage. As the full discovery of the character continues, adjustments may need to be made. Within the parameters of the production, directors should allow actors latitude and support inspiration.

## SEARCH FOR THE CHARACTER'S HOOK

A *hook* is a repeated gesture, phrase, movement, or sound that epitomizes the character. It is the singular expression that most identifies the character to the guest. If guests remember one thing about the character, this would be it; if they mimicked the character to their friends, they would use this trait. It may be a phrase like Archie Bunker's "Stifle!" Homer Simpson's "Dough!" (which was actually Alan Hale's hook as the captain of the SS *Minnow*, on "Gilligan's Island"), Scarlett O'Hara's "Fiddle dee dee!" or Fred Flintstone's "Yabba dabba doo!" It may also be a quirky habit or gesture like Chaplin's tramp twiddling his mustache and swinging his cane, Rodney Dangerfield's tight collar, or even W. C. Fields' characteristic draaawl.

A hook is important because, as the name implies, it *grabs* you, and makes you take notice and remember. It makes a unique statement that fits the uniqueness of the character.

A strong hook is a powerful tool, but it is not so much designed as discovered. It is most often the product of a moment of inspiration while playing the character. Nonetheless, an awareness of what a hook is, and an attitude toward finding one, can help cultivate that moment of inspiration. Actors should not be distressed if they don't find their hook right away; it is sometimes found only after the character is played for a while.

## DEVELOP A CHARACTER SIGNATURE

A *character signature* is a combination of sound, movement, gesture, or phrase (such as a motto or axiom) that signifies the character to the actor. This signature can be used in performance when the characterization begins to slip away, or when the actor's concentration is off. It is much like a hook—it can even *be* the hook—but is significant only to the actor. A signature may have no obvious meaning at all to anyone else, but must "say it all" about the character to the actor. Repeating this "personal hook" reestablishes the character to the actor and renews his or her belief in and commitment to the characterization.

A colleague of mine played a character he called the Oaf quite expertly and for many years. He was known for his absolutely unshakable commitment to the character. He used this idea in what he called his "character mantra." He devised a little song that always made him *feel like the Oaf.* Whenever he felt his concentration slipping in performance, he would find a tree or bench to march around and quietly sing his "Oafy song" to himself. The lyrics of the song were nothing more than the word "Oafy," repeated over and over again. It not only helped the actor regain his focus, but also allowed guests to see the Oaf do the kind of entertainingly silly behavior one might expect of an oaf.

### DEVELOP A BYLINE

Each character should have a *byline.* A byline is a short expression that explains the character's occupation and attitude toward it. It is given when they introduce themselves in performance. If the character's occupation is not identifiable to the guest as the character approaches, this expression nails it. A good byline can even reveal the character's passion or foible.

My 1940s Hollywood character ensemble at Disney–MGM Studios had some good examples, such as the incompetent gumshoe—"Willie Ketchem, finest private detective in Hollywood"—and the naïve and talkative girl off the bus: "Hi, my name is Elsie White, I just got off the bus, but I should be a big movie star in about an hour." The model characters from *The Art of Play* might choose the following bylines: the ambitious prospector, "Eustus Panfreed, soon to be the most upstandin' member o' this here town"; or the dim-witted, novice outlaw, "I'm Notorious Ned, and ya better be scared or I'll shoot ya."

Bylines should never seem forced; they should fit with the character and make sense for the situation. The best opener to any cold contact with a guest is an endowment (covered in the next phase), but whenever an introduction is used, the byline provides the character exposition needed to get an interaction going.

### DEVELOP A RITUAL FOR GETTING INTO CHARACTER

At this stage in development, insist that actors make getting into and out of character a deliberate act. It doesn't matter what they do to get into character. They don't need a lot of hocus pocus, they just need to take a moment to quiet themselves and *acquire* the character. Likewise, they should not casually drop the character when they are through with an exercise or performance, but should again take a moment to consciously set the character aside.

There are a myriad of mental distractions in interactive performance, and actors must avail themselves of every crutch to maintain their character's integrity. This simple discipline of mentally marking where the character's life begins and ends helps condition the actor to commit to the character. I allow them to be in character, or out, but never halfway.

I later ask them to take this discipline a step further and develop a set *ritual* for getting into and out of character for performances. For example, as they put on their costume, they think of it as *putting on the character*. They might dress in the same way and in the same order each time. Or they may groom, dress, and apply makeup through the character's eyes. Maybe they stay in character from then on, or just use that time as a private exercise in reviewing the character's elements and semblance. Their ritual may also include their character signature. This technique utilizes sense memory to help the actor get into character quickly and completely. Once actors develop their ritual, they should never vary from it.

## Character Interviews

PURPOSE: To give actors an opportunity to bring together all of their character choices and to experience them as a whole.

DESCRIPTION: A chair is placed in the center of the room, and one by one, each character takes the chair for a five to ten minute interview. The focus of these interviews is "getting to know the real you." The instructor, acting as interviewer, may ask all of the questions or take questions from listeners. The character interviewed remains in character at all times and answers each question spontaneously, whether they had considered the topic previously or not. The interview environment is a safe environment, not a third degree. Characters are to answer freely, and without reservation or fear of retribution, any question asked of them.

NOTES: 1. The instructor should make sure basic questions are

covered, such as background and professional life, then continue with more probing or even obscure questions.
2. The questioning should be well paced, but when short answers are given, the character should be asked to explain "why."

COMMENTS: Character interviews are most useful in the early stages of development after choices have been settled. They allow the actor to experience the character in a very detailed way, without the additional complexity of scene work. It is also an excellent way for ensemble members, and the director, to become familiar with new characterizations.

## Group Character Interviews

PURPOSE: To allow actors to experience their character choices in relation to other characters.

DESCRIPTION: Group character interviews are conducted in the same manner as *Character Interviews*, except that three to five characters are interviewed at once. This small panel of characters may be asked questions individually, or may each be asked to respond to the same question. Interaction among the characters on the panel is allowed, but the main focus must remain on the current interviewee.

NOTES: The interviewer should keep things moving, but follow up on any reactions based on interplay between the characters.

COMMENTS: If the Character Interview exercise is a Barbara Walters interview, then the Group Character Interview is a Geraldo Rivera interview.

## Party Scene in Character

PURPOSE: To unite physicality, character choices, and relationships in a full cast environmental scene.

DESCRIPTION: The instructor marks off the main components of a party scene, using whatever rehearsal furniture is available. The party takes place within the period of the production, and the instructor motivates it, so that any character of the

ensemble would have reason enough to be there. A cast of
characters are let loose upon the scene, and all share the same
objectives: first, to introduce themselves and get to know each
other person in the room, and second, to pursue their occupational needs.

NOTES:   1. From time to time, call out highlights of the party, to
keep it interesting and active, such as "Dinner is
served" or "The police have arrived."
2. Actors are bound to preserve their physicality and
the integrity of their characterizations, no matter
what the action of the scene.
3. Actors must never speak in groups larger than three.

COMMENTS: Obviously, this exercise incorporates many aspects
of interactive performance, from language and physicality styles
to good scene work. It does not involve the most important
aspect of interactive performance: the guest. However, it can
help actors to become comfortable with their characters and
their interactions within the ensemble.

## Party Scene in Character—Variation

PURPOSE: To provide a venue for characters to get to know
each other, and to become more in touch with character establishing information.

DESCRIPTION: This exercise proceeds just like the Party Scene
in Character exercise, except that none of the characters know
each other. Their objective for the scene is to introduce themselves to, and get to know, each other character at the party.
Even characters with previously established relationships are to
behave as if this were the moment of their first meeting.

NOTES: Actors must note that the kind of information they are
constantly giving out in this exercise is the same information
sought by guests, who are meeting them for the first time.

COMMENTS: Some characters are designed to be unacquainted
with other characters each time the performance begins, and
others are not. However, even though some characters have
long-standing relationships, this does not diminish the necessity
of establishing those relationships for the guest. All too often,

actors internalize previous performances and reveal less and less to the guest as time goes on.

## Need-Oriented Scenes

PURPOSE: To explore using the character's primary needs to create action.

DESCRIPTION: Two actors perform a scene in character. Before the scene, Player One chooses one of his/her primary needs to explore in the scene. Player Two supports that need. The focus of the scene is arriving at new action to fulfill P1's needs. P2, though not pursuing his/her needs in the scene, must nonetheless support P1's needs in a way that is natural for the character.

COMMENTS: Need-oriented scenes offer an opportunity to develop a supportive relationship between ensemble characters. Obviously, when characters work together they cannot both be pursuing their character needs at the same time. In addition, need-oriented scenes can inspire many new ideas for character Lazzi and encounters.

BELIEVE IN THE CHARACTER

In order to make the audience believe the character, the actor must believe the character. Have the actors develop a personal relationship with their characters. Allow them to get to know their characters as they would a good friend. Suggest they perform the character when they're at home, while driving, cooking, shopping, etc. Encourage them to get to know how it reacts to certain things like cameras, children, handshakes, fire hydrants, and cigarettes. The actors should strive to make the character another person in their lives.

## Dinner in Character

PURPOSE: To experience the character in a real-life situation.

DESCRIPTION: Actors form small groups, leave rehearsal in character, and go to a public restaurant for dinner. They are to remain in character the entire time and react as the characters would react, come what may (short of anything dangerous, illegal, or immoral). For characters deemed too extraordinary for the public eye, a dinner party can be created.

COMMENTS: Having to react in character to real-life situations will force the actors to make quick decisions on how their character will react, and will give them a true sense of spontaneity. It will also test their commitment and belief in the character by creating a situation with higher stakes than the rehearsal hall can offer. Imaginative instructors may find other real-life situations to visit in character.

## Scruples in Character

PURPOSE: To develop the character's values and attitudes.

DESCRIPTION: In this exercise, the cast simply plays the popular game "Scruples," only they play it in character. In dealing with the morality-teasing questions of the game, actors must come to grips with their character's values, morals, and attitudes. In addition, they will learn a great deal about other characters, through the discussion the game engenders.

NOTES:  1. The instructor must strongly emphasize that actors are to follow their character's values, not their own personal values. Follow the character!
2. Actors must present their character's philosophy in a strong and confident manner during the game, whether or not they ultimately adopt it.

COMMENTS: This exercise can be quite informative and extremely enjoyable when played after rehearsals in a comfortable setting.

### DEVELOP A PERSONAL MYTHOLOGY

As the actor's relationship with the character builds, so too should the character's relationship with the environment they will live in. Start giving the character opportunities to relate to the performance environment. They should build memories, histories, and experiences attached to specific locations in the environment. I call this the character's *personal mythology*. (The ensemble's *group mythology* is covered in the Performance phase.) Use these exercises to connect the character to the environment.

## Characters Explore Environment

PURPOSE: To connect characters to the Performance Environment.

DESCRIPTION: This is a "private" exercise where characters are left to explore individually the actual performance environment that will be used for the production. They are to connect the characters to the environment in two basic ways. The first is by knowing the space. Characters must walk every inch of the performance space. They should walk the extreme perimeter and crisscross every open space in a number of different directions, making it as familiar to them as their own living rooms. Second, they must attach themselves emotionally to the space. For each area or set piece they approach, they must decide what importance, if any, that area has for their character. They should consider the following: How familiar is the character with that space? How does that aspect of the environment affect or relate to their occupation? What emotional attachments or memories are associated with that part of the environment? (For instance, "On this spot I met my first love," or "In this building I lost my job," or "At this place I regularly meet my friends," etc.) In addition, characters may incorporate into their thinking any group mythology developed during the rehearsal process and any overriding scenarios for the production.

NOTES:  1. Characters should remain in character, think like the character, and see the space through the character's eyes.
2. Actors should be encouraged to touch everything they can reach, and sit, stand, or climb on anything that is safe for them to do so.
3. Characters may talk to themselves, verbalizing their musings in character.

COMMENTS: This exercise is absolutely essential and should be repeated as often as necessary, and as early as the production schedule permits.

## Tour of Environment

PURPOSE: To explore the character's personal mythology within the performance environment.

DESCRIPTION: The full group divides into pairs: Player One plays his/her character and Player Two plays the role of a guest. Beginning and ending at the same point, P1's character gives P2, the mock guest, a tour of the environment. This tour is conducted through the eyes, experience, and attitudes of the character. Characters should reveal to their guests what each place means to them. They might point out their favorite places, historic information, personal opinions, and gossip engendered by each location they pass. On completion of their tour, actors switch roles. P2 then plays his/her character, giving a tour to P1's mock guest.

NOTES: Mock guests may ask questions and probe the character for a deeper understanding, but they should limit conversation to the environment and the character's relationship to it.

COMMENTS: This exercise is an extension of the Characters Explore Environment exercise, but adds the layer of revealing this information to the guest.

## The Character's Favorite Space

PURPOSE: To connect the character with the performance environment through a favorite spot.

DESCRIPTION: Characters are set loose upon the actual performance environment and asked to find their character's favorite space. This is the one space within that environment that the character feels most comfortable in, or perhaps has the fondest memories of. Once it is found or decided upon, characters are allowed to linger in the space and consider what it means to them and how it makes them feel.

COMMENTS: The character's connection to this place may be useful during performance, when the actor needs to reconnect to the character. It also presents the actor with a psychological touchstone for the character, knowing that their favorite place is close by. It will engender a more positive relationship between the character and the performance environment.

## Scene Work in Character

Begin Scene Work in Character about halfway through Advanced Character Development. Keep exercises going in conjunction with scene work until the character is well "seated" in the actor's psyche. This is important because there is a great tendency for improvisers to discard or alter their characterization to what will get an immediate reaction in the scene. Hopefully they have been trained out of playing for themselves in a scene, and this will help. It will take some time before they are as comfortable improvising with their created character as they would be with an off-the-cuff character. They should know and expect this. Once established, their interactive character will afford them many more options that will be more grounded and real than "instant characters" can provide.

Up till now, the improv training has not been applied to interactive performance. Scene work in the abstract is different from scene work with an established characterization. (See Chapter Fourteen of *The Art of Play.*) They will expand their understanding of the character through using it in scene work, and adjust their improv technique to deal with more givens. In interactive performance, the "where" and "when" variables are absolute and unchangeable. If the production is set in Vulture Gulch, Colorado, 1885, then it must remain so. The location cannot be altered for the sake of an interesting scene. The character, although flexible, must also remain the same character created for the production. Therefore the "who" is largely unchangeable. What must be developed is *relationship*, or who the character is to another. In addition, the *action of the scene*, or "what," must be developed, and the "why," or *motives of the action*, must be pursued.

Don't confuse an established variable with establishing the information in the scene. Although the "who," "where," and "when" are established in the *production*, the actor must still established them for the *audience*, or else they do not exist.

For in-character scene work then, the actor must establish for the audience the predetermined who, where, and when, and create the what and why. In-character scene work explores relationship and character motives; it reveals the character's passion and foibles and creates here-and-now action that can involve the guest.

At this point, the guest's place in the scene is set aside until interactive technique is covered in the Technique phase.

Nonetheless, careful attention should be paid to the creation of guest-inclusive activities in the scene work. This is the main goal of characters improvising with characters. (See Active Choices, page 119.) Establish this habit here, so that the ensemble will not become too used to playing for each other and later ignore the guest. There are, of course, hundreds of ways to initiate scene work, such as choosing variables and situations. Below are a few that will utilize many characters at once, conserving rehearsal time.

## Ben's Chili Bowl

PURPOSE: To practice using character elements and explore character relationships.

DESCRIPTION: This scene takes place at Ben's Chili Bowl restaurant (or a restaurant of your choice). Tables and chairs are set up within the rehearsal space so that there are only two seats to every table, and the seating capacity of the restaurant is several short of the total number participating. This requires some to stand at the door and wait for a free table. The exercise begins with all tables being filled with pairs of actors facing each other. This diner-style restaurant places patrons who don't know each other at the same table, and explorative conversation is the result. Actors play their characters, chatting over their imaginary bowls of chili, and get to know one another. Each character uses his/her chosen needs as a touchstone to their behavior. After a brief tête-à-tête, characters walk to the door, leaving their table completely free for the next two patrons. Characters vacating a table go to the end of the line at the door, where the instructor acts as maitre d', seating new patrons. Each time a character is reseated, it is with a different character. The instructor calls, "Closing time at Ben's!" when most or all have had a tête-à-tête with everyone in the group.

NOTES:  1. Actors are asked to accept the convention of a restaurant regardless of whether it fits in the context of the show being produced.
2. Coach lines include *"Follow your needs!" "Listen to and respect the needs of others!" "Build a relationship!"*

COMMENTS: The context of chatting over a light meal allows

actors to explore their characterizations without being overly concerned about physicality and action. It is best performed before heavy scene work in character begins.

## Visiting Characters' Homes

PURPOSE: To explore character relationship and character detail.

DESCRIPTION: One character enters their "home" and takes some time to define the space. The visiting character enters, is greeted warmly, and is shown about the place. After this tour is completed, the character-at-home chooses to share an object or activity with the guest. The scene concludes when the visiting character leaves the performance space.

NOTES: 1. Visiting characters may have a previous acquaintance with the character-at-home.
2. The visiting character rejects nothing, but graciously accepts any offer.
3. The visiting character initiates closure for the scene by motivating his or her exit.

COMMENTS: One of the ways we as human beings galvanize our relationship to others is by taking them to our home and showing them our stuff. This exercise has equal importance in deepening the actors' understanding of their characters, since we know ourselves through our surroundings and through our relationships with others.

## ABC Scenes

PURPOSE: To provide practice for scene work in character.

DESCRIPTION: A location is chosen for the scene. Player A and B enter the space and begin a scene in character. Once a premise is developed, Player C enters the scene with a supporting assumption. As soon as that assumption is established and incorporated into the scene (this should not take long), Player A motivates an exit and leaves the scene (B and C should assist A in motivating the exit). The scene continues until Player D enters the scene with another supporting assumption. Upon the establishment of that assumption, B then motivates an exit and leaves the scene. This process continues until the full group has played through the scene.

NOTES:  1. The location should be one within the actual performance environment. The location does not change as the ABC scene develops.
2. The amount of time when there are three actors in the scene should be brief, and at no time should there ever be more than three.
3. Actors should be coached to keep the scene active and not allow it to degrade into a "talking heads" scene.

COMMENTS: ABC Scenes is a workhorse structure that allows many characters to interact at one time. It is also good for practicing good second support and establishing motivated exits. I have had as many as seven ABC scenes running at once in the same room, where actors exit one scene, then enter another, and so on. For clarity and added interest, I will sometimes place a coin in the performance space and decree that the coin must be passed from character to character in a motivated way, and always remain on stage.

## Image Scene in Character

PURPOSE: To practice general scene work in character, with an emphasis on focus.

DESCRIPTION: Player One enters the performance space, defines the location, and motivates his or her character's presence in it. As soon as this is established, Player Two enters with an assumption that heightens the action. P1 incorporates the assumption into the scene. As soon as that is done, Player Three enters with a new assumption that heightens the action even more. P1 and P2 incorporate the assumption into the scene. This process continues until the scene is filled with six to eight characters. The last character's assumption is solved, and the character that presented it motivates an exit to the scene. Thereafter, characters solve the problem their assumption created, in reverse order, and motivate their exits. The scene concludes with P1 motivating an exit from the space.

NOTES:  1. Each new problem should be more serious than the

preceding ones. Early problems should start small so that the scene may have build.

2. Actors in the scene must lend focus to each entrance and exit, and help to incorporate the new assumptions into the scene.

COMMENTS: This scene can be a lot of fun, but it requires good concentration and focus to succeed. Remind actors that scenes with this many characters are rarely effective in performance, but they provide an excellent challenge in rehearsal and help build mutual support.

ACTIVE CHOICES

*Active choices* are how the primary activities of the character are translated into meaningful, active play with the guest. An actor must look for ways to make active choices for each primary activity. As scene work in character begins, present the idea of active choice and begin workshopping with the actors for each of the character's Primary Activities.

An active choice is an *outward activity that requires immediate action or involvement from the guest in order to be fulfilled.* It is outward and physical, not contemplative or cerebral. (See Chapter Fourteen of *The Art of Play.*) The main qualities of an active choice are as follows:

- An active choice is an outward activity.
- An active choice is a here and now action.
- An active choice includes the guest.
- Active choices connect the actor to the guest through *need.*

## Active Choices

PURPOSE: To explore active choices.

DESCRIPTION: An actor chooses a character activity, then makes an active choice using the ensemble as mock guests. Afterward, point out its active or inactive nature, then ask the ensemble for supporting suggestions. Here are some examples from the Wild West model:

**Not an active choice**: Annie Trueheart, Mail-Order Bride, needs help finding her husband. She asks a male guest, and he answers, "He went that-a-way." Annie thanks him, tells him that she is a mail-order bride from Boston, and goes off to find her intended husband.

**Active choice**: Annie asks a male guest for help finding her husband. He answers, "He went that-a-way." Annie thanks him and asks, "What does he looks like?" She then gets to explain that she is a mail-order bride and has never met him. But since the guest obviously knows him, she makes him describe him . . . and to her liking. Perhaps he must stand like him, walk like him, talk like him. In the end Annie proposes marriage to the guest instead.

COMMENTS: It takes a fair amount of rehearsal and experience to pick up the knack of making an active choice. It is easier for actors to simply perform the activity themselves. They must learn to break this habit in favor of finding ways to manipulate the activity so that the guest's actions bring about the desired result.

Active Choices Log
Using the form on the following pages, actors should keep a log or journal of their choices.

## *Background*

Once the essentials of the character are well rooted in the actor's psyche, it is time to flesh out the details of its existence. (See Chapter Nine of *The Art of Play*.) The sheets on the following pages make a handy reference for these details. Actors should write in pencil, and be willing to erase if better choices present themselves. They must realize, too, that these specifics must yield to the greater good of the scene if a guest's assumption preempts them. As they develop these backgrounds, actors should endeavor to establish this information in their scene work. There are three components to character background:

- *Personality:* These are factors of innate personality, aspects of nature that the character was born with and that remain unaffected by any developmental factors.
- *Childhood Development:* These are purely developmental factors, aspects of the character's childhood and adolescence that helped shape the character.

## Active Choices Log

Catalogue three active choices for each of the top ten primary activities of the character. Describe them in detail, and comment on (a)
how the subject, occupation, and passion of the character are
revealed and (b) how the foible might affect the outcome. Active
choices are actions between the character *alone* with the guest(s).
The "active" in "Active Choice" refers to the *guest* being active.

**Activity #____:** _____

*Active Choice 1.* _____

_____

_____

_____

    a. How are subject, occupation, and passion revealed? _____

    b. How might foible affect outcome?_____

*Active Choice 2.* _____

_____

_____

_____

    a. How are subject, occupation, and passion revealed? _____

    b. How might foible affect outcome?_____

*Active Choice 3.* _____

_____

_____

_____

    a. How are subject, occupation, and passion revealed? _____

    b. How might foible affect outcome?_____

■ *Professional Life:* This outlines the current life situation of the character.

These background factors must not be developed before this point in the process. If chosen too early, background detail will tend to limit the actors' view of their character before they have a chance to experience it fully. Actors must resist the urge to create a backstory for a character whose essence is still to be formed.

Some background information may need to be predetermined in an interactive play, but this should be done only when needed to justify a plot line or necessary action.

A vocabulary of attitudes is also included here to help actors find the words to describe their creations.

## Personality

These are factors of innate personality that the character was born with and that remain unaffected by any developmental factors.

### 1. Appearance:

**Age** (child, young, adolescent, youthful, mature, middle-aged, old, ancient):_____

**Grooming** (dirty, clean, unkempt, immaculate, rough, ragged, plain, attractive):_____

**Stature** (erect, hunched, shriveled, tall, imposing, slight, squat, floppy):_____

**Movement** (quick, slow, fluid, sharp, sluggish, halting, disjointed, rhythmic, graceful, heavy, plodding, agile, brisk, bustling, nimble, vigorous, sprightly, lively):_____

**Dress** (sloppy, immaculate, elegant, glamorous, meticulous, well-groomed, dirty, simple, ragged):_____

**Speech** (soft, harsh, musical, pleasant, grating, loud, raspy, sexy, squeaky):_____

2. **Disposition and Tendencies Toward Others** (optimist, pessimist, helpful, mischievous, trusting, suspicious, obsequious, arrogant, friendly, abrasive, blunt, courteous, compassionate, insensitive, humble, proud): _____

3. **Intellect** (dull, average, active, dreaming, ponderous, antiintellectual, scheming, brilliant, adroit, ingenious, keen, quick, smart, mindless):_____

4. **Nature** (soft-hearted, forgiving, hard-hearted, unforgiving, jealous, vengeful, kind, gentle, fickle, affable, devoted, loving, sociable, loyal, genial, affectionate, amicable):_____

5. **Energy** (lazy, energetic, driven, eager, animated, zealous, intense, vigorous, ardent, sprightly): _____

6. **Honesty** (scrupulous, honorable, truthful, lying, deceitful, righteous, genuine, fair, pious, true, insincere, false, shallow, inconstant, hypocritical): _____

7. **Materialism** (generous, covetous, greedy, avaricious, miserly, mean, thrifty, spendthrift, wasteful):_____

8. **Will** (gullible, weak, strong, unshakable, decisive, determined, insecure, indecisive, subordinate, pliable):_____

9. **Idiosyncrasies:** _____

10. **Habits:** _____

**11. Gestures and Mannerisms:** _____

_____

**12. Carried Props:** _____

_____

## Childhood Development

These are purely developmental factors, aspects of the character's childhood and adolescence that helped shape the character and may have an effect on current behavior.

**Parent(s) Name(s):** Mother_____ Father_____

**Siblings:**_____

**Parent(s) Occupation(s):** Mother _____ Father_____

**Dwelling** (rural or city, of what construction, address, size, any persistent odors or sounds?):_____

_____

_____

**Economic Status** (destitute, poor, changeable, average, well-off, wealthy, other): _____

_____

**Hobbies or Interests:**_____

_____

What *was* your attitude toward other classes of society?_____

_____

_____

What *was* more important to you than anything else while growing up?_____

_____

_____

What special skills did you acquire while growing up?_____

_____

_____

Describe your feelings toward your childhood experience._____

_____

_____

Describe any ambitions you had. _____

_____

_____

Describe your fondest moment as a child. _____

_____

_____

## Professional Life

This outlines your current life situation.

**Name:**_____ **Age:** _____

**Profession:**_____

**Dwelling:**_____ **Social Position:** _____

**Economic Status** (destitute, poor, changeable, average, well-off, wealthy, other):_____

_____

**Possessions:**_____

_____

_____

**Values and Beliefs:** _____

_____

**New Interests:** _____

_____

**Attitude Toward Other Classes of Society:**

    Upper:_____

    Middle:_____

    Lower:_____

**Vices:**_____

_____

**Influential Friends** (if any): _____

_____

**Skeletons** (actions or acquaintances you wish to hide): _____

_____

_____

What are your career goals? _____

_____

Are you successful in your profession?_____

What is your attitude toward your profession?_____

_____

What skills are required?_____

_____

How are others involved?_____

_____

What is your greatest fear?_____

What was the biggest moment of your life?_____

_____

_____

## A Vocabulary of Attitudes

*Attitudes chiefly rational:* Explanatory, instructive, didactic, admonitory, condemnatory, indignant, puzzled, curious, wistful, pensive, thoughtful, preoccupied, deliberate, studied, candid, guileless, thoughtless, innocent, frank, sincere, questioning, uncertain, doubting, incredulous, critical, cynical, insinuating, persuading, coaxing, pleading, persuasive, argumentative, oracular.

*Attitudes of pleasure:* Peaceful, satisfied, contented, happy, cheerful, pleasant, bright, sprightly, joyful, playful, jubilant, elated, enraptured.

*Attitudes of pain:* Worried, uneasy, troubled, disappointed, regretful, vexed, annoyed, bored, disgusted, miserable, cheerless, mournful, sorrowful, sad, dismal, melancholy, plaintive, fretful, querulous, irritable, sore, sour, sulky, sullen, bitter, crushed, pathetic, tragical.

*Attitudes of passion:* Nervous, hysterical, impulsive, impetuous, reckless, desperate, frantic, wild, fierce, furious, savage, enraged, angry, hungry, greedy, jealous, insane.

*Attitudes of self-control:* Calm, quiet, solemn, serious, serene, simple, mild, gentle, temperate, imperturbable, nonchalant, cool, wary, cautious.

*Attitudes of friendliness:* Cordial, sociable, gracious, kindly, sympathetic, compassionate, forgiving, pitying, indulgent, tolerant, comforting, soothing, tender, loving, caressing, solicitous, accommodating, approving, helpful, obliging, courteous, polite, confiding, trusting.

*Attitudes of unfriendliness:* Sharp, severe, cutting, hateful, unsociable, spiteful, harsh, boorish, pitiless, disparaging, derisive, scornful, satiric, sarcastic, insolent, insulting, impudent, belittling, contemptuous, accusing, reproving, scolding, suspicious.

*Attitudes of comedy:* Facetious, comic, ironic, satiric, amused, mocking, playful, humorous, hilarious, uproarious.

*Attitudes of animation:* Lively, eager, excited, earnest, energetic, vigorous, hearty, ardent, passionate, rapturous, ecstatic, feverish, inspired, exalted, breathless, hasty, brisk, crisp, hopeful.

*Attitudes of apathy:* Inert, sluggish, languid, dispassionate, dull, colorless, indifferent, stoical, resigned, defeated, helpless, hopeless, dry, monotonous, vacant, feeble, dreaming, bored, blasé, sophisticated.

*Attitudes of self-importance:* Impressive, profound, proud, dignified, lofty, imperious, confident, egotistical, peremptory, bombastic, sententious, arrogant, pompous, stiff, boastful, exultant, insolent, domineering, flippant, saucy, positive, resolute, haughty, condescending, challenging, bold, defiant, contemptuous, assured, knowing, cocksure.

## *Improv Narrative Skills*

Continue refining the improv technique in the morning improv sessions. Improv here should still be done in the abstract so that the actor can focus completely on the technique. As techniques are learned here, they should show up in the Scene Work in Character workshops as well.

Below are exercises for most of the important prescripts for conducting an improvised narrative. (For a full discussion of these points see Chapter Thirteen of *The Art of Play.*) Beyond the sharing and building of ideas in improv scene work, these techniques ensure good dramatic form and style. They include the following:

- The best way to establish an assumption
- The importance of addressing the who, what, and where of a scene
- Observation and memorization
- Keeping the action on stage (coached)
- The problems of canceling the action (coached)
- Breaking the routine
- Reincorporating assumptions (coached)
- Making motivated exits
- Techniques for creating closure

ASSUMPTION EXERCISES

## Sentence at a Time

PURPOSE: To recognize the essential elements of a narrative. To learn to listen to and accept the ideas of others. To practice memorization.

DESCRIPTION: A group of four to twelve players stand in a circle facing inward. Player One begins a narrative by giving one complete sentence only. The player to the right adds the next sentence, and so on. Play continues around the circle until each player has gone twice. By the time the last player provides his/her last sentence, the story must have come to a reasonable conclusion, with all loose elements tied together.

NOTES:  1. Players must focus on listening to the story, rather than developing possible responses in their heads before their turn. If they do not listen and absorb the story as it is being told, they will not be able to add constructively to the narrative.
2. Actors must focus on not dropping any information from the scene. Likewise, whatever information is established cannot then be negated.

COMMENTS: In this exercise, players learn that there is a time in a narrative for building information, a time for conflict, and a time for resolution. It will train the actor's eye toward the development of the whole story, and not merely their "role" within it. It emphasizes the importance of listening rather than predetermining responses. It is also good practice in memorization; facts, names, places, and events must be remembered in order to be brought together for the ending.

## Story, Story

PURPOSE: To support and develop a narrative. To respond spontaneously. To focus on listening.

DESCRIPTION: Four to six players stand in a line facing their conductor. A topic is chosen for a story, and the conductor uses a baton or finger to point to one of the players, indicating that he or she should begin the story. Player One begins a spontaneous story, speaking for as long as the baton is pointed at him or her. The conductor moves the story along by simultaneously cutting off one player and cueing another. The new speaker must pick up where the other left off; whether it be in midsentence or midword. Players cued must continue the story without pause or stumbling, without repeating a word, and remaining syntactically correct. Players cut off must not run over. When players break any of these rules, they are given a point by the conductor (or observers). The conductor indicates when the story should be wrapping up, and the players themselves arrive at the ending, concluding with the words "the end." Points are tallied at the end of the story to see who did best. (Another version excludes players from the group whenever they break a rule. The story is concluded when there is only one player left.)

NOTES: 1. The players watch the baton and focus on understanding the story. Trying to anticipate where the story is going, or plan a response, will only spell disaster.
2. The conductor should begin by letting each player establish an uninterrupted assumption; this gets the narrative going. Afterward, they should cut in sooner, and more often in midthought.
3. To make cuts sharp and clear, alternate hands, dropping one pointer as you bring up the other on a new player.

COMMENTS: This exercise accomplishes much of what "Sentence at a Time" does while adding a greater challenge to spontaneity. It is an excellent exercise for developing cooperation, spontaneity, and narrative skill.

## Half-wit Narrated Story

PURPOSE: To develop a narrative spontaneously from more than one source of information.

DESCRIPTION: Players One and Two form a half-wit (see Half-Wit exercise on page 66) and act as narrator to a silent scene that will be played by Players Three and Four. A character relationship and location is chosen for the nonverbal scene. P1 and P2, as half-wit, stand offstage and provide narration and dialogue for both P3 and P4. P3 and P4 act out the narration and dialogue, adding actions of their own, suggested by the scene. The half-wit players use any information P3 and P4 add to the scene through their physicality. The result is that P1 and P2 respond spontaneously not only to each other, but to what is being developed by P3 and P4.

NOTES: Players three and four follow unfailingly the narration of the half-wit, although they are to embellish it, using gestures and actions of their own design.

COMMENTS: This exercise accomplishes a lot all at once: give and take, listening, relinquishing ideas, judgment, and cooperating toward the attainment of a cohesive whole.

## Image Scene

PURPOSE: To develop a narrative using the physicality of other players, and to reinforce focus and listening skills.

DESCRIPTION: Player One and Player Two begin a scene. At an appropriate point in the scene (one with good physical interest), the instructor calls "freeze." At this point one player from the group immediately enters as a "real-time narrator." A real-time narrator is actually present in the scene's reality, but still does not take part in the action. The narrator uses the physical freeze as their "flash" for the new scene: a new whole reality justified by the freeze. The narrator narrates the action of the new scene.

P1 and P2 develop the scene from the narrator's information, now nonverbally, embellishing it physically as they see fit. The narrator utilizes any physical information provided by P1 and P2. The instructor again calls "freeze," whereupon all three players are now frozen, and a new narrator, Player Four, enters the scene. P4 incorporates the physicality of *all three* for a new scene. This process continues with a new narrator being added each time "freeze" is called. This exercise concludes when the full group is involved in the scene.

NOTES: 1. The narrator must never take part in the action of the scene, only narrate.
2. Entering narrators must make no hesitation but immediately take charge.
3. As the number of players within the scene increases, so should their sensitivity to the narrator's information. For instance, if the narrator says "one monkey danced," players must be careful not to respond with a scene made entirely of dancing monkeys. One may assume the role of a trainer, others of observers, etc.
4. Players are also free to develop a split focus for the scene. For instance, two players in the group observing the monkey dancing may suddenly develop a marital argument, which the narrator may then choose to use to further the scene.

COMMENTS: This is a great exercise for developing a facility for creating assumptions, and with group give-and-take. As the number of players increases, the requirements for focus and listening also increase. The exchange of ideas between narrator and nonverbal player creates great opportunities for creative cooperation. *Variation*: At the end of the series of scenes, they are replayed in reverse order. Narrators resume their original narration, and conclude it before the next freeze.

WHO, WHAT, WHERE EXERCISES

### Who, What, Where, in a Minute

PURPOSE: To develop skills in "planting" the scene, i.e., establishing the who, what, and where.

DESCRIPTION: Two players are chosen for a one-minute scene.

No variables are given, such as location, place, or character relationship. The two players begin a scene and must establish, in as clearly and detailed a way as they can, the who, what, and where of the scene, before the one-minute time limit is up.

NOTES:  1. A player must not "script" the scene by attempting to give all of the necessary information alone. They must build the who, what, and where together.
2. Coach players to *Take the time you need! Don't rush it! Cooperate! Relax! Listen! Work together! Be specific!*

COMMENTS: Players should soon find it quite easy to establish the who, what, and where in a minute. Then play two different scenes within one minute, with the timekeeper calling "change" at the thirty-second mark, then three twenty-second scenes within a minute. This is an excellent exercise to train actors to establish information clearly, specifically, and early.

## Screenwriters

PURPOSE: To practice verbalizing the *where*, and making specific and descriptive assumptions.

DESCRIPTION: Two players seat themselves in the playing area. They agree on the *who*, *what*, and *where* of the scene. Players approach the scene as two screenwriters describing the climatic scene of a motion picture to producers, through narration and/or dialogue, but no action. They play out the scene verbally for the group, much like a radio play. Players are to focus on describing in acute detail every physical nuance of the scene that reveals the where. For example:

Player One: "Rick found Susan strangled there in the dank cave. Her soft body thrown hard against the dark, slick rocks of the cave floor. Drops of water falling out of the darkness above pelted his raincoat. There is something else in the musty air, the smell of danger. 'So it's you.'"

Player Two: "Rick was suddenly aware of me standing behind him, the revolver sweating in my palm. 'Yeah, it's me. Put your hands up.'"

NOTES:  1. Players must strive always to give a detailed picture of the where through sight, sound, smell, touch, and taste.

2. Coach players to *Stay in the present! Describe! Be specific! Verbalize objects that show the where! Stay actional!*

COMMENTS: Actors tend in improv to center mainly on action, secondarily on character, and least of all on location. This exercise forces them to take the time to establish a clear where. It is also a good exercise for training actors to be specific in their assumptions. Using descriptive language adds more meaning to assumptions and gives the opposite player more to associate with.

OBSERVATION AND MEMORIZATION EXERCISE

## The Memory Game

PURPOSE: To increase an actor's capacity for memorization.

DESCRIPTION: The group pairs off. Player One makes a long list of objects, then reads a list of seven objects to Player Two without pause. Once the list is read, P2 immediately begins counting out loud from one to fifteen, and then immediately repeats the list back to P1, who scores the number of correct answers. This is then repeated with eight objects, then nine, and so on. When P2 can no longer repeat back the full list, players switch roles and repeat.

NOTES: The player memorizing should attempt to place a key with each object as he hears it. A key for "stapler" may be visualizing it on one's desk at home. A key for "rag doll" may be the letter R made out of red rags, etc.

COMMENTS: A good memory is essential in improvisation simply because facts must be remembered in order to be reincorporated later into the scene. Another good memory game involves a player walking into a room full of objects and being given a certain amount of time to memorize as many objects as he or she can. Upon leaving that room, players list as many as they can remember.

BREAKING THE ROUTINE EXERCISES

## "Ding" Scenes

PURPOSE: To develop spontaneity in making assumptions and breaking the routine.

DESCRIPTION: Two players begin a scene (variables may be chosen). At a point just after a player makes a new assumption in the scene, the instructor rings a bell or calls out the word "ding." At that point, the player instantly inserts a different assumption. Replayed assumptions should always repeat the first few words of the previous assumption, for example:

Actor A: "Look, Captain, that's the biggest fish I've ever seen!" *Ding!* ". . . that's the biggest boat I've ever seen!" *Ding!* ". . . that's the biggest jerk this side of the Mississippi." The scene continues as if only the newest assumption had been said. The instructor continues to "ding" players at will. The scene ends when an appropriate closure is found.

NOTES:  1. The instructor may present single or multiple "dings."
        2. Players must never break character while being "dinged" and must always endeavor to disguise any angst or loss for words.

COMMENTS: This exercise not only helps actors become more spontaneous in their scene work, but helps them become more familiar with breaking the routine. It helps them see how easily seemingly disconnected material can be incorporated into the scene so that it makes sense. This should make them feel more comfortable with being immediate, and with offering the extraordinary.

## Extraordinary Assumptions

PURPOSE: To practice making assumptions that offer high stakes or break the routine.

DESCRIPTION: Player One stands in the performance space. All remaining players (Two, Three, Four, etc.) line up offstage. Player Two enters the scene and delivers an extraordinary assumption to Player One (i.e., "So you've started a revolution," "It's Armageddon time again, God," or "You're my long-lost mother!") P1 makes a single responding assumption (one sentence only) to P2, and P2 exits to join the back of the line offstage. One at a time the remaining players then enter with extraordinary assumptions for P1. When P2 is once again at the beginning of the line, he or she takes P1's place in accepting assumptions. P1 joins the end of the line. Another round of extraordinary assumptions is then begun by P3, at the end of which P3 takes P2's place, etc. This continues until all players have had their turn responding to extraordinary assumptions.

NOTES:   1. Remind players that extraordinary assumptions make listeners wonder what happens next and precipitate heightened or unusual action.
2. The exercise should move along very quickly.

COMMENTS: This fast-paced exercise can help the actors break away from the mundane and become comfortable with putting their characters in peril.

MOTIVATED EXIT EXERCISE

## Motivated Exit

PURPOSE: To develop awareness and support of entrances and exits in a multicharacter scene.

DESCRIPTION: A team of five to seven players choose variables for a scene. Two players begin the scene while the others stand on the sidelines waiting for a second support entrance. The scene progresses with characters entering and exiting the scene at will, provided two conditions are met. First, any player entering or exiting the scene must provide an assumption that properly motivates the entrance or exit, and second, all other players in the scene must lend their complete focus to each and every entrance or exit made. The scene ends when a natural conclusion is reached.

NOTES:   1. Players' motivating assumptions must fit with the scene. For example, in a scene where someone faints, a motivating exit might be, "I'll go find some smelling salts." Or, in a scene where a party is being held, a motivating entrance may be a pizza delivery.
2. If the instructor or audience observes any entrance or exit that is not supported by all players, that player is called back until focus can be acquired.

COMMENTS: The more characters in a scene, the more difficult the focus is to handle. This exercise requires an actor to have a reason for entering or exiting a scene. It also requires an increased sense of ensemble and mutual awareness, since players must acquire full support before making their entrances or exits.

CLOSURE EXERCISES

## First Line, Last Line

PURPOSE: To practice developing closure.

DESCRIPTION: Two players take the stage for a scene. The instructor or observing group calls out the first and last lines to be spoken in the scene. Players begin a scene inspired by the first line, then work together to motivate the scene to a place where the last line provides closure.

NOTES: 1. The first and last lines chosen should be as dissimilar as possible in order to give the players somewhere to go.
2. Players are responsible for repeating the chosen lines verbatim.

COMMENTS: This exercise gives actors an overall objective for the scene that both players are aware of and must work toward together. For this reason it is also a good structure for getting actors to cooperate and support each other.

## Title Scenes

PURPOSE: To develop good closure habits.

DESCRIPTION: Four teams of two are formed. An interesting and complete title is obtained from the observation group, such as "The beasts of the forest rise up against the elves of Los Angeles." Each team, in turn, does *the first half* of a scene based on the information suggested by the title. These four scenes may at first have no obvious connection to one another. When Teams One through Four have all entered the space and done the first half of a short scene, the order is then reversed, and Teams Four through One play out the *endings* of their scenes. The second round of scenes both conclude themselves *and* connect with the previous scene(s). The final scene, by Team One, ties all the scenes together.

NOTES: 1. It is wisest for each team to choose one or two elements within the title to develop. For example, Team One might develop the idea of "elves of Los Angeles." Team Two may establish "the beasts of the forest," Team Three a conflict between them, etc.
2. They may either exit or remain on stage at the end of each segment.
3. Continuity must be maintained within each team's scene, and the overall scene.

COMMENTS: This structure is complex and may take some practice, but once understood by the players, it provides a wonderful challenge to their ensemble skills.

## Scenario Rehearsals

Scenarios are usually character dependent and are impossible to rehearse before characterizations are formed. They may be a group of performance elements for an interactive event, or the single guiding story of an interactive play. Either way, characters should now be formed enough for them to begin. A block of rehearsal time should therefore be set aside and used throughout the remainder of rehearsals for their development. (See Chapter Fifteen of *The Art of Play.*)

# *Technique* 6
# *Phase*

With characters fully activated, narrative skills covered, and scenario rehearsals opened, begin discussion and exercises in interactive technique, build endowments and lazzi, and continue with advanced improv skills.

## *Interactive Technique*

One of the more difficult, and certainly the most contrived, phases of rehearsal is teaching interactive technique without guests to work with. Nothing in the rehearsal hall will ever compare to working the guests of an actual performance. Still, the best way to teach and practice audience-interactive techniques is to use "mock guests" in rehearsal.

The difficulty is to find actors who can portray guest reactions realistically. The tendency is for actors to *act*. In playing guests, they play a *role*, instead of just playing themselves. Even an actor's natural reactions tend to be a bit showy. Many will try to make themselves "guests from hell," for the sake of being dramatic. Experienced interactive actors can often draw on their experience to create fairly realistic guests. A little coaching on the sidelines from the director can help a great deal. I will give mock guests very specific objectives to play, and provide parameters for their reactions, such as "You are a married couple in your thirties, new to an interactive show, but open to it, curious and willing to play; you will make some offers, but would not try to take over the scene." In general, mock guests are far more challenging than most real guests. New actors should know that if they can work with mock guest reactions, they will find the real ones much easier.

For exercises where you want to use the environment, it is useful to split the ensemble in two, one half to play mock guests and the other to play characters (then switch). For workshop exercises, choose small groups of actors to play mock guests as in the Guest Scenes exercise below.

You may consider using nonactor volunteers as guests in rehearsal, but I have found these even less useful than mock guests. The trouble is that these nonactors are very conscious of themselves, and become very unnatural. They are far less able to respond to direction, and tend to slow things up.

Use the section on Interactive Performance Technique as a guide. (See Chapters Sixteen through Twenty of *The Art of Play*.) Start by workshopping some of the basic concepts covered in "Relating to the Guest" and "Street Staging." Then place the players in as many mock guest situations as you can, and illustrate techniques in "Creating Interaction," "Playing the Bit," and "Tools of the Trade," as situations arise. This will give them an experiential connection to the technique and will be far more effective than merely teaching it and giving examples.

The cast may get good and tired of playing to each other as guests. This is not necessarily a bad thing. It will work to the ensemble's benefit to be eager to see a real audience rather than apprehensive about their first interactive performance. The more prepared they are, the better their performance will be. Rehearse them *past* the point of it feeling new and exciting. The performance will be plenty exciting when they get to it, and they will be ready to capitalize on it.

### Guest Scenes

PURPOSE: To explore and exemplify good interactive technique.

DESCRIPTION: A location from the actual performance space is chosen (use actual space if possible). One actor enters the space in character, and begins *passive lazzi.* The instructor selects one or more actors to play guests and sends them into the scene with specific objectives or attitudes likely to be encountered from guests during performance. Some examples: a young couple interested and anxious to play with characters; a husband and wife with a shy child; a group of adults uncertain about their role in interacting with a character; teenagers in a peer group. The actor's objectives are *to engage the guest, inspire interaction*, and *react positively to the guest's behavior*. The scene ends when the character closes the scene or when the guests decide to move on. At the end of each scene, the instructor points out the good choices that were made and discusses how other choices might have been made better. Another character is chosen and a new guest scene begins.

NOTES:  1. Actors playing guests should be strongly encouraged to play the ordinary, to play themselves and resist the temptation to be "on."
2. The instructor should send in guests that range from the easy to the "moderately challenging," and not make a point of tripping up the actor.

COMMENTS: Guest scenes are admittedly contrived. The instructor should point out that these scenes do not represent a true performance experience. However, they can inspire informative discussions and useful examples of both good and bad choices.

## Guest Environment

PURPOSE: To explore interactive technique within the performance environment.

DESCRIPTION: The full cast splits into two equal groups. Group One portrays mock guests, and Group Two portrays their interactive characters. Both groups roam the performance environment and engage in a mock production. Before the exercise, G1 may be given specific mock guest types to perform. As the exercise continues, the instructor may choose to call out different performance elements for G2 to explore, such as character action, endowments, lazzi, or encounters. The exercise continues until stopped by the instructor. G1 then plays their characters, while G2 portrays mock guests, and the exercise is repeated.

NOTES:  1. Coach actors on all aspects of interactive technique, such as street staging, creating interaction, and playing the bit.
2. Remind mock guests to remain spread out among the environment and to let the characters come to them; otherwise both groups will tend to clump near the center.
3. Make no physical delineation between mock guests and characters. If the difference isn't clear, then character physicality needs to be heightened.

COMMENTS: This mock performance will give the actors as close a feel for the production itself as is possible without actual guests. Pointing out good and bad technique will be more effective after this exercise, since actors will be better able to relate to the experience.

## Developing Character Lazzi and Endowments

Developing elements is an ongoing process of performance, but it is started in rehearsal by writing and workshopping. The idea here is to build an arsenal of lazzi and endowments for the actor to try out as the show opens. Some of these rehearsal-made elements will succeed and some will fail, but it is best to be prepared. After opening, the process is one of weeding out the bad, capitalizing on the good, and always striving to create more.

### GUEST ENDOWMENTS

An endowment is an invitation to the guest to play along, by bestowing upon them a role to play in the production or scene. Every character must have its own stock of endowments to throw on guests. In this phase players begin through writing and workshopping to develop their stock, which is then refined and expanded as the performance run continues. These endowments exist only for each character; they are not shared by other characters in the ensemble. They make up a unique set of people in that character's life, as though they were characters of a sort of "personal novel." They will become very familiar to the actor, and they will develop over time. (See Chapter Fifteen of *The Art of Play*.) I have actors keep a log of these characters in what I call their Endowment Zoo.

The Endowment Zoo begins with listing guest "targets." The target is the type of guest commonly encountered in performance for which an endowment might be designed. Sample types include an elderly couple, a single male adult, a teenage girl, a child under twelve, a crying baby, etc.

Once an endowment is designed for a target, it may be repeated for every target of the same type. This allows the actor to present a more detailed and well-thought-out endowment to the guest. As the endowment is repeated, refinements can be made to make it as effective as possible. Obviously, the same endowment would not be thrown twice in the same proximity of guests. You would not want a guest to hear you using the same character to another guest. To prevent this, more than one endowment character can be devised for a given target, or just improvise a new one. Many new endowments happen this way.

Have actors use their character's primary needs and activities as a springboard to creating endowment characters. They can start by asking themselves what their character needs, then who in the character's world would be able to fulfill that need.

Actors can use a sheet like the one on the next page to record their endowment characters. By performance time, several dozen should be written and memorized. Writing during the rehearsal process means creating without the aid of performance experience, but a list must be in place before opening. After opening, the log should constantly be refined and added to, as the actors see what works best for them. An actor can acquire quite a few endowment characters over time.

A good endowment answers the following questions:

*Who*
**Name.** A proper name should be established for every endowment character. Also include *your* character's name and byline if you can.
**Background.** This includes their occupation, history, and importance to your character. Remember, every endowment character is an "important person."
**Relationship to your character.** Does your character know them personally or by reputation? Have an attitude toward them.

*What*
**What does your character want from them?** This should be an urgent or high-stakes want.
**What does the endowment character have to do?** A here-

and-now action is best. Will other guests be needed to accomplish this task as well?

**What will your character do to get what he or she wants?**
Consider the stakes. How far will your character go? (They must be willing to lower their status.)

*How*

**How does this want fill your character's need?** You reveal your character's needs through your endowments, and so reveal your character.

**How does this want relate to your character's occupation?**
This want should engender activities within the realm of the character's occupation.

### Endowment Zoo

**Target Group:** _____

**Description:** _____
_____
_____

**Relationship:** _____
_____
_____

**Active Need:** _____
_____
_____


**Target Group:** _____

**Description:** _____
_____
_____

**Relationship:** _____
_____
_____

**Active Need:** _____
_____

## You Have, I Want

PURPOSE: To focus on need and endowment in scene work.

DESCRIPTION: Player One has a need that can only be satisfied or supplied by Player Two. P1 *wants it*, P2 *has it*. At the beginning of the scene, only P1 knows the need. The scene starts with P1 endowing P2 with the quality or situation of having it. P1 must acquire the need at any cost, but cannot name it until P2 makes it clear that he/she knows what it is. P2 may resist giving it to P1, but only within what is reasonable and motivated for the scene. P1 must raise the stakes until his or her want is satisfied. Actors then switch roles and choose a new want.

NOTES:  1. This exercise can be played out of character, or with P1 in character and P2 as a guest.
2. P2's role is to raise the stakes for P1. When P2's character would reasonably be convinced, P2 grants P1's desire.
3. Actors must realize that their power in this scene lies not in mere pleading or refusing, but in *endowing* their partner or themselves with new information that broadens the context of the scene.

COMMENTS: The essential action of this exercise is creating endowment characters, in much the same way as they would be created for guests. In each case, the character has a strong need to fulfill, and creates an endowment for the partner (actor or guest) that has the power to fill the need. The artistry comes with creating interesting action for its fulfillment!

## Endowment Reception Line

PURPOSE: To practice throwing endowments.

DESCRIPTION: The entire group forms two parallel lines facing each other. Player One finds the partner, Player Two, standing directly across from them. With their lists of endowment characters in hand (see the Guest Endowments section), P1 endows P2 as an endowment character from his or her list (in character). P2 then endows P1. When finished, P1 then approaches the actor to P2's right and continues with another endowment character from P1's list. Likewise, P2 moves to the actor to P1's right. The effect is that of a wedding reception line, where each member is endowed with a different character from the actor's list. Actors reaching the end of their line simply flip over to the opposite line and continue in the opposite direction (the image of a rolling tank tread may help here). The exercise concludes when the instructor calls a halt. At this point actors should have exhausted their endowment list at least once.

NOTES:  1. Endowments are graciously accepted before moving on.
2. The actor's objective is both to memorize and to improve the efficiency and effectiveness of their endowment.

COMMENTS: This exercise is mere practice for using the endowment characters devised by the actor. They must be fully internalized if they are to surface in the spontaneity of performance. Another very useful version requires actors to *improvise* all their endowments. This is a brain bender, but it can produce many new ideas.

### BUILDING LAZZI

*Lazzi* is a collection of simple actions, gestures, or phrases that reveal character and can be easily worked into any circumstance. A *lazzo*, (singular form) should have reliable comic content and a clean close. (See Chapter Fifteen of *The Art of Play*.)
    Good lazzi accomplish the following:

- Give the effect of surprise or laughter
- Reveal the extraordinary nature of the character (their occupation, passion, and foibles)
- Involve the guest in as active a way as possible (i.e., they include an active choice)
- Inform the guest about the subject and theme, or relate to the overall scenario

There are a number of ways actors can search for lazzi. One of the least useful is sitting around waiting for inspiration to hit. An active creative process will yield much more fruit. Here are some ideas.
    As a prelude, always hold the character in its entirety in your mind. Consider all its needs and foibles, its passion and back-

ground, etc. See it in performance successfully entertaining guests. Maintain a comic attitude about it; try to see life from a different point of view. Think well of your creation and yourself.

Peruse your occupational activities list (see the form on page 59). See the character performing the activities in the environment, and to the delight of the audience. Relax your mind and play with the activities. Look for a simple action, gesture, phrase, or a combination that gives surprise and/or laughter to the guest, in a way that only the character could.

Try relating your primary activities list to your primary needs. (See the Character Elements List on page 59.) See your character performing a primary activity as motivated by a primary need. Select a combination of one primary activity and one primary need, and try to imagine a lazzo. Then move on to another combination, then another, until all are exhausted.

Look at primary needs in relation to a foible. See the character pursuing its need and the foible as a deterrent to its fulfillment. How can this manifest itself physically? Use the juxtaposition of foible and need to create comedy. Look at primary activities in relation to the foible in the same way. Select a specific combination and consider it well before moving on.

Use your fellow ensemble member's imagination. Have him or her use some of the above creative techniques to come up with lazzi for your character, while you do the same for your partner.

Lazzi generally involve a single character and guest, but sometimes characters are paired up for much of the performance, like two detectives working on a murder case. *Two-character lazzi* can be devised for characters on the same side of an activity, so to speak. (Characters on opposite sides of an activity, such as a starlet auditioning for a director or a man proposing to his girl, are really developing action, and would therefore be in the realm of an *encounter*.) Abbott and Costello would share two-character lazzi when Abbott slapped Costello or hit him with his hat.

## Walk Through a Day

PURPOSE: To explore character activity in order to develop lazzi.

DESCRIPTION: Actors make a priority list of five activities from their primary activities list. Characters spread out among the performance environment (or a mock-up using chairs and tables). Placeholders for guests should be created as well, if possible. (Music stands work well for this.) Characters imagine themselves at home and begin their day as the character normally would. They then leave their home, and travel to the performance environment. Once there, they pursue the first primary activity on their list. The actors' job is not to plan out their activities, but to follow the character and live in the moment. As they encounter imaginary guests, they endeavor to involve guests in their activity. They may visualize any response they wish from their imaginary guests, and let their imaginations rule. When they are satisfied that their imaginary guests have physically participated in the activity, they may close the scene and move on. They then choose the next primary activity on their list, and seek to fulfill it elsewhere in the environment. Actors are to make written notes of any new discoveries for character lazzi.

NOTES:  1. Characters may not speak or react to any other characters in the environment, only to their imaginary guests.
2. Coach actors to *Follow the character! Follow the activity! Don't think, react!*

COMMENTS: This quirky exercise has yielded many new ideas for character lazzi. If actors commit to their imaginations, they can actually see and interact with their imaginary guests. The contrivance of a physical placeholder for imaginary guests is a device I have added, because some actors find it difficult to be consistent with the guests they visualize. Having an actual physical focus may seem silly, but it really helps.

*Lazzi Log* ■ Actors should maintain a log of their character's lazzi on a form like the following:

## Lazzi Log

Lazzi Description:_____

_____

_____

Lazzi Description:_____

_____

_____

CONCEITTI

*Conceitti* are short, written monologues designed to display the character's particular brand of pretension or hubris. They are tirades of boastful self-importance or righteous passion. The Dottore in the commedia dell'arte would often "go off" on a barely intelligible stream of philosophical dogma or scientific jargon. The Lovers were wont to lose themselves in a lavish description of their love for each other. These were totally premeditated, highly emotional comic jags, and were used, like lazzi, when invention failed or opportunity knocked.

The fact that they are scripted is excused by the fact that they are short tricks used only to embellish the scene. They require no dialogue or interaction. They are of minor importance as performance elements go, but are handy tools for actors to carry in their bag of tricks, to bring to bear when the time is right. Use conceitti to reflect the character's attitude on a topic of importance to them, or their worldview. (See Chapter Fifteen of *The Art of Play*.)

Actors should keep a log of their conceitti. The following form might prove useful.

### Conceitti Log

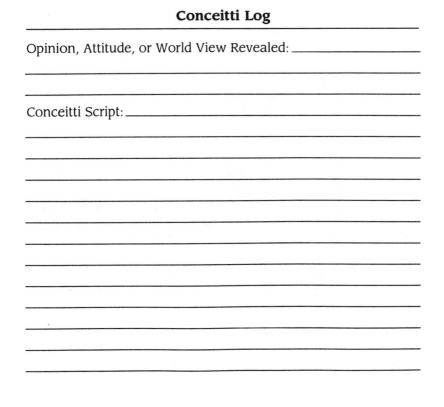

Opinion, Attitude, or World View Revealed: _____

_____

_____

Conceitti Script: _____

_____

_____

_____

_____

_____

_____

_____

_____

_____

_____

## *Advanced Improv Skills*

It is a good idea to keep up improv workshops throughout the rehearsal process. A good deal of in-character improv is happening at this phase, but improv skills may best be honed through continued abstract improv. These exercises do not use the actors' interactive characters. Here the focus is all on the improv technique and not on the development of the interactive character. Below are some scene structures I have found to be quite useful in advancing improv technique. Many are harder than they appear to bring off well. Work them beyond mastery, to perfection. Be sure to point out any insights that apply to character work in the production.

### Coached Scenes

PURPOSE: To practice all aspects of good improvisation technique.

DESCRIPTION: Two actors take the stage for a scene (variables may be given). Second support from the observing group is allowed. In coached scenes the instructor merely calls out coach lines on any aspect of good improvisation, whenever they are needed. Despite coach lines being given, actors are required to continue the scene unless the instructor calls, "Freeze." When freeze is called, the scene stops for a more detailed coaching, then resumes where it left off.

NOTES: 1. Any and every kind of coaching is allowed for this scene, e.g., "Focus!" "Listen to each other!" "Establish your where!" "Move it forward!" "Where's the closure?!" etc., etc.
2. The instructor must always phrase the coaching in positive terms and remain at all times supportive of good technique, not critical of bad technique!

COMMENTS: In these scenes, the instructor acts as a crutch or a *conscience*, if you will, for each performer to maintain good improv technique.

### Scene Tag

PURPOSE: To translate a frozen physicality into a new scene.

DESCRIPTION: The full group divides into teams of six to twelve players. Players One and Two begin a scene (variables may be chosen). Other players line up along the sidelines. Once the scene is established, the next player in line, Player Three, searches for an appropriate freeze point, one where there is an interesting physicality. When it's found, P3 calls out, "Freeze," and immediately approaches the two frozen players. P3 then taps one of them out of the scene (literally taps them on the shoulder), and assumes that chosen player's physicality as precisely as possible. The tapped-out player goes to the end of the line offstage, and the tapping-in player is responsible for beginning the new scene. The new scene must be a whole new scene, not a continuation of the previous scene, and must somehow be based on, or "justify," the physical freeze of the two players. Alternative versions include the instructor calling the freezes, or having players who see a good opportunity call "freeze" and emerge from the line in any order.

NOTES:  1. Scenes should be kept fairly short, less than a minute, before a freeze takes place.
        2. Freezers are wise to search for interesting physicality.
        3. The new scene must always justify the physicality.

COMMENTS: Scene Tag is an excellent exercise for initiating and establishing scenes. It provides a good opportunity to rehearse positive assumption, building character, and action. It is also helpful in ensemble work since it provides players a chance to do scene work with many other players in a short time.

## Five Through the Door

PURPOSE: To develop quick decisions and commitment, by establishing different characters.

DESCRIPTION: The full group divides into teams of five to seven players; each team plays separately. Player One is chosen as the head of the complaint department for a business such as a department store or used car dealer. This person takes a position on the stage as though seated at a desk; other players are lined up along the sideline. The first player in line, Player Two, enters by opening an invisible door. P2 enters with a distinct characterization, and has a specific complaint for P1. P1 quickly solves P2's problem. P2 exits through the doorway, then immediately turns around and enters as another distinctly different character, with a new complaint. P1 satisfies P2, who exits again, and immediately returns as a third character, and so on. With the fifth complaint complete, P1 goes to the end of the line, and P2 assumes P1's role as head of the complaint department, and P3 now performs five characters through the door. This process continues until all players have played all roles.

NOTES:  1. "Through the Door" characters must be as dissimilar as possible; variety counts.
           2. There should be no hesitation or stalling before reentering. The actor must decide quickly, and commit to the character.
           3. The complaint department person merely responds to the character's complaint, without initiating a complex scene.

COMMENTS: This is a good exercise for actors to practice stretching themselves in snap characterizations. It is of particular use with stage improv, but can also help broaden an actor's sense of possibilities during interactive character development.

## Beginning, Middle, End Scene

PURPOSE: To focus on ensemble, understand scene structure, and not drop assumptions.

DESCRIPTION: Three teams of two are chosen, and each takes its own place in a line on the stage. Variables are chosen for a scene involving two characters. Each team plays the *same two characters* throughout the scene. Team One will only portray *the beginning* of the story (establishing information, foreshadowing, etc.). Team Two portrays *the middle* of the story (rising conflict, new problems, etc.). Team Three portrays *the end* of the story (resolution of conflict). Only one team performs at any one time, by stepping forward and playing a portion of the story. After a brief scene (just a small portion of story information is given) the team steps backward, leaving the stage open for another team to step forward. The next team must incorporate any previous team's information into its part of the story. (For example: The *middle team* presents a scene where the two characters are flying an airplane and suddenly run out of gas; the *beginning team* may next portray one character's interest in learning to fly.) Teams present their portions of the story in random order. The exercise is finished when a natural conclusion is reached by the *ending team*.

NOTES:  1. Teams should be cautioned never to drop an assumption presented by another team. All assumptions must be incorporated into the whole story.
2. Subteams not performing should concentrate on listening and understanding the scene being portrayed, rather than on trying to plan their next scene.
3. The initial scenes of each team should create a broad space of time and action, and should *not* seem to be related to each other. The progression of scenes must bring the disparate parts of the story together to form a whole.
4. Each individual team's "*scenelets*" are chronological in order, even though there may be great gaps of elapsed time.

COMMENTS: This structure can get quite complex, especially for the middle team, which is trying to assimilate information from both sides. Once the players are comfortable with the structure, it is an excellent way to train them to listen to and incorporate the assumptions of others. In this particular scene advance planning or scripting will spell disaster. It will be very obvious to all when a particular actor is forcing his or her own ideas into the scene, rather than following the flow of ideas in a spontaneous manner.

## Who Am I?

PURPOSE: To focus on communicating through behavior.

DESCRIPTION: Teams of two players prepare as in Endowments with Player One exiting the room and Player Two choosing, with the group, one occupation for P1 and another occupation that P2 will use for the scene. P1 enters with an assumption (guess), and P2, using gibberish only, attempts to endow P1's occupation upon him/her. (P2's occupation is used only as grounds for action in the scene.) The exercise is over when P1 correctly guesses his/her occupation by using it in an assumption.

NOTES:  1. Players must not allow the exercise to become a

game of charades. Players must create a scene using
P2's occupation, and work within the context of that
scene.
2. If P1 cannot guess, P2 should make his or her
endowments more and more obvious.

COMMENTS: In an alternative version of this game, P2 discards
the gibberish and speaks normally. Who Am I? is a somewhat
simpler version of Endowments, and is recommended before
Endowments is attempted.

## Endowments

PURPOSE: To focus on communicating information through
behavior rather than dialogue.

DESCRIPTION: Two players are chosen for the scene. Player
One leaves the room while Player Two and the full group
choose three variables: *P1's occupation, a room in a house,* and
*an object* belonging to P1. P2's objective in the scene is to
endow this information on P1 in such a way that P1 may
"guess" the variables. P1 guesses by playing out behaviors
rather than shouting them out as in a game of charades. P2
speaks only in gibberish; P1 speaks normally. P1 must continue
making assumptions as "guesses" while listening to and accepting the endowments made by P2. (For example, if P1's occupation is dentist, P2 may begin the scene by sitting in a chair and
opening his mouth. If P1 guesses correctly, he or she may say,
"Open wide, we have to drill that cavity. As your dentist I'm
appalled at your brushing habits.") The last piece of information
to be endowed must be the object. When P1 correctly guesses
the object, P2 is to somehow "kill" P1 with the object, ending the
scene.

NOTES:  1. P1 should initially enter the scene with a strong
assumption as a wild guess.
2. The room in a house chosen as variable need not be
the location of the scene. P2 may choose to travel to
that room to make it more obvious.
3. The instructor may wish to impose a time limit for
the scene, adding pressure to P2 to be clear and precise in his or her endowments.

COMMENTS: Endowments can be an enjoyable structure, creating many comic moments when P1 guesses incorrectly. It also forces players to communicate by their behavior rather than rely on language.

## Emo Spot

PURPOSE: To incorporate emotional levels into a scene spontaneously.

DESCRIPTION: Emo spot, or "emotional spotlight," involves two or three players. An additional player is an emotional conductor. The conductor makes a list of emotions (the observing group may help), and stands to the sidelines. Players begin a scene. The conductor calls out various emotions from the list, which must then be incorporated into the action of the scene. The conductor may call out an emotion for *any* player, or just a particular player. The scene ends when it comes to a natural conclusion. (A fun variation is Emo Zones, where emotions are assigned to zones taped on the floor that the players move through at will, taking on the emotion of the zone they are in.)

NOTES:  1. Emotions called for by the conductor need not be maintained by the players until the next emotion is called.
2. The conductor should choose emotions that will make the scene more interesting.

COMMENTS: This is a standard structure for stage improv. In addition to emotions, "Spot" scenes may also involve theatrical styles, movie genres, literary authors, languages, etc.

## In a, With a, While a . . .

PURPOSE: Incorporating three variables into a scene.

DESCRIPTION: An ample list of the three variables required of the scene is made. Variables must fit syntactically into the sentence, "This scene takes place in a (blank), with a (blank), while a (blank) is happening." (They are essentially choosing a location, an object, and an action for the scene.) Once the list is made, the instructor chooses one variable from each column, and two or three players take the stage to play out the scene.

They play the scene to a close, but within a time limit specified by the instructor.

NOTES: The variables need not be established in any particular order, but they must be established before the end of the scene.

COMMENTS: This is an interesting set of variables with which to establish a scene. The goal here is good scene work, not merely establishing the variables. Therefore, an interesting premise must be arrived at, developed, and closed.

## Expert Endowments

PURPOSE: To practice finding the premise or context of a scene.

DESCRIPTION: Expert Endowments runs just as the Expert exercise (see page 68) does, except that the expert is unaware of what he/she is an expert on. The interviewer knows the area of expertise, and must pursue a line of questioning that requires specific answers from the expert without revealing the expert's area of expertise. When the expert "guesses" the area of expertise, he or she makes it obvious within the normal line of questioning and the scene is over. Players then switch roles. The topic of expertise is chosen by the interviewer with the help of the observation group.

NOTES:  1. The expert is to always appear calm and confident in his or her knowledge of the topic.
2. The interviewer must find ways of requiring specific information from the expert without revealing the topic. If the scene runs long, the interviewer may become more obvious. The idea is to challenge, not stump, the expert.

COMMENTS: In any improvised scene, actors must "read between the lines" and agree upon the premise of the scene. This exercise places one player in the position of having to agree with the details before knowing the context. It also provides a great focus on developing the appearance of confidence and assurance in an improv situation.

## Hidden Obsession

PURPOSE: To develop communication and subtext in scene work.

DESCRIPTION: One team of two players takes the stage for a scene. Variables may be chosen, such as character relationship and location. Player One also chooses a hidden obsession. This obsessive bit of behavior is somehow connected to Player Two, such as being obsessed with touching P2's hair, or seeing what's in P2's pocket. P1's objective is to satisfy the obsession without P2 ever being aware of it. If P2 guesses it, P2 confronts P1 with the obsession. The scene is over when the hidden obsession is either guessed by P1 or obtained by P2.

NOTES:  1. Both players must maintain their focus on developing an interesting scene, allowing the obsession to be purely subtextual.
2. P1, the obsessive player, may attempt to motivate the scene in such a way that it becomes easier to satisfy the obsession, but both players should be extremely careful not to negate or deny the other player's assumptions.

COMMENTS: This is a great exercise for showing actors that information and character can be revealed on more than one level at the same time. This can add great interest and fascination for an audience. It can also add an air of suspense that will maintain an audience's interest.

## Gib (Gibberish) Translation

PURPOSE: Focus on give and take.

DESCRIPTION: Two teams of two players are chosen. Team One takes the stage while the members of Team Two sit to either side of the performance space facing the players. T1 performs a scene in gibberish only (variables may be chosen for this scene). Each player in T2 takes on the task of translating the gibberish for one of the players on stage. The scene progresses as though it were a foreign film being dubbed for English.

NOTES: 1. Translators, T2, are only to translate gibberish initi-
ated by their player on stage; however, they may
interpret that gibberish any way they wish.
2. Gibberish players, T1, add inflection to their gibberish, and provide information to translators through
their physical activity in the scene.

COMMENTS: This is an excellent structure for give and take.
The gibberish players feed information in the form of inflection
and action, the translators feed information through language,
and the scene works when cooperation is achieved.

## Internal Narration

PURPOSE: To reveal the internal workings of a character's mind
within the scene.

DESCRIPTION: Players One and Two take the stage to begin a
scene (variables may be given). Player Three stands on one side
of the stage and acts as P1's internal narrator, likewise, Player
Four stands on the opposite side of the stage and acts as P2's
internal narrator. Internal narrators voice the inner, *true*
thoughts of the characters. The scene begins, and at appropriate
points in the scene, an internal narrator claps or makes a "ding"
sound. This stops the action and allows that narrator to speak.
As the internal narrator speaks, the character may react appro-
priately. When the internal narration is over, the scene resumes,
and that information is incorporated into the action.

NOTES: 1. During narration, characters are not frozen like stat-
ues; they may subtly react to what is said.
2. Character/narrator partners "feed" each other, to set
up interesting action.

COMMENTS: The interest in these scenes relies heavily on a
good give-and-take relationship.

# *Performance Phase* 7

*W*ith an understanding of interactive technique, and some good endowments and
lazzi developed, begin developing character
relationships, mythology, and encounters.
Certainly by now from their work since the Development
phase, the ensemble has a feel for how their characters
relate. This "feel" must now be clarified and put into context
with the production. Along with relationships, the production's mythology must now be solidified. Last, but far from
least, encounters must be created. These form the back-
bone of the interactive production, but they can only be
properly developed when all the other rehearsal phases are
complete. All of these items may be started as soon as
Technique phase items are well under way. Don't get
caught with too little time for these; it is better to start them
too early than too late.

## Building Character Relationships

Always remember that the reason for having established
relationships between characters is to either *further a necessary plot, reveal a theme,* or *create interesting interaction*

*with guests*. Guide all your efforts to these three ends, and don't get mired in the details. Use relationships as a springboard to these goals, not as a ball and chain that limits action. Don't set them in stone, set them in mud. However well ingrained in the actor's performance habits a relationship is, and no matter how successful or emotionally attached to it the actor has become, there are two irrevocable rules about character relationships for interactive theatre:

- Relationships do not exist until played for the guests at hand.
- Unless established in the scene already or necessary for plot development, the actor's preconception of relationship must change in favor of a guest's assumption or the greater good of the scene.

Character relationships can sometimes be more gratifying to the actor than guest relationships, because actors play along more competently than your average guest. Care must be taken not to focus on relationships with other characters to the exclusion of guest endowments. Like a good soap opera, character relationships can be so engrossing for the actors that they lure them away from good interactive technique.

## Roundtable Relationship Discussion

PURPOSE: To provide discussion of character relationships.

DESCRIPTION: The full cast sits in a circle, forming a "round table" for discussion. This exercise simply presents a forum for actors to hold a brief discussion with each other actor about how their characters might relate to one another in performance. Player One speaks with Player Two (to P1's right in the circle) about how his or her character may feel toward P2's character. P2 may provide feedback on how his or her character may feel about P1's character. P1 then moves to Player Three, and on around the table in a counterclockwise direction. When P1 has discussed character relationship possibilities with each other actor in the circle, the discussion moves to P2. P2 then begins a similar discussion around the table, then P3, and so on, until all actors have completed a roundtable discussion. (As the discussions proceed around the table, overlapping discussions are skipped, so that by the end of the exercise each actor has spoken with each other actor only once.)

NOTES:  1. Outline what points the discussions should follow, e.g., occupational common ground, personality differences, situations for interesting conflict, use of guests.
2. The instructor should prompt discussions, keeping the exercise moving along.

COMMENTS: This exercise is not as complicated as it sounds, although it does take several hours. It is, however, time well spent because it gives a comprehensive view of the landscape of relationships within the ensemble. Actors are often inspired by individual ideas for character work, as well as by the clarity this exercise gives to their character's position within the citizenry of the show. Remind actors to take notes!

## Character Attitude Toward Characters

PURPOSE: To develop character relationships.

DESCRIPTION: Players pair up. Player One writes a list of five attitudes his or her character might have toward his or her partner's character. Player Two does the same. They then discuss how their characters might interact in performance. When finished, P1 and P2 pair up with other actors, and continue the process until every actor has a list of five attitudes for every character in the production.

NOTES: Actors' initial choices may be tempered by their discussions with their partners.

COMMENTS: This exercise forces actors to be specific about how they relate to each other in performance. The objective is to create a relationship with an interesting dynamic for the guest, which will feed actors with interesting possibilities for action.

## Group Character Interviews—Variation

PURPOSE: To further explore character information and to develop relationships.

DESCRIPTION: This exercise proceeds as the Group Character Interviews (see page 109) exercise does, except that the interviewer is also a character.

NOTES:  1. The interviewing character motivates the reason for the interview, and must establish each character's name and occupation.
2. Further questions by the character interviewer may be biased toward that character's own interests.
3. The character interviewer maintains control throughout the interview, and his/her authority is supported by each interviewee, at all times.

COMMENTS: This twist adds a stronger focus on character relationships, and can help to define a character's own values and opinions.

## Description of Characters (in Character)

PURPOSE: To sharpen an actor's knowledge of other characters in the ensemble.

DESCRIPTION: Player One steps before the group and, in character, describes an undisclosed character in the ensemble. P1 may employ any appropriate bias toward the unnamed character; and describe this character physically, mentally, and emotionally, as well as what he/she means to P1. They also should make ample use of metaphor. (See Metaphor Description exercise on page 64.) By the time P1 is through with the description, it should be clear to all who the character is. The character is named, and that actor then steps before the group. This continues until all have described another character, in character.

NOTES:  1. Remind actors not to make eye contact with the unnamed character.
2. Actors should be encouraged to employ any creative means they feel their characters might use to describe the unnamed character.

COMMENTS: This exercise is not only useful during the rehearsal process, but also as the production itself develops and the characters evolve. Understanding of fellow characters and their relationships can become murky as time goes on. This exercise can help keep those perceptions up to date.

## Social Station Lineup

PURPOSE: To establish the hierarchy of social station within the cast of characters.

DESCRIPTION: Actors are asked to line up in order of social station, from highest to lowest. They are to place themselves where *they* believe they belong in the line. When they have gone as far as they are able without dispute, the instructor intervenes and completes the hierarchical lineup. Actors inspect the lineup and use it to determine initial dominance in their encounters.

NOTES: Do not let actors dispute their social station for long. Intervene and determine it yourself. Some social stations are very close, nonetheless, form a single line.

COMMENTS: The fascinating thing about this exercise is some actors' immediate ego involvement and resentment toward certain characters being higher in station than their own. It may surprise you how many actors take this personally. It is an excellent opportunity to point out their subjective emotional attachment to their character's dominance. If actors cling to their selfish notions of social station in this exercise, they are likely to cling to a selfish dominance in scene work. The purpose of the exercise is to establish a clear pattern of *initial dominance*, but will provide the instructor with an opportunity to point out that the value of dominance lies in how it *changes*, not in how it *begins*.

# Building a Mythology

The *mythology* is the sum of the facts, histories, and relationships "known" by the ensemble prior to the beginning of the performance. It is the backstory of the production, the collective relationships of characters to each other and to their environment—the body of information that all of the ensemble accepts as given when the show commences.

The intent of a mythology is twofold:

- To give the illusion of a detailed reality
- To give the actors a starting place for their improvisations

Building mythology is a fascinating endeavor. As you help your cast create it, be aware that actors may fixate on the mythology of the show to the exclusion of interaction. In making this background detail, some unplayable action will be created. Keep them focused on how the mythology can be used in performance to create action or reveal character. It doesn't matter that one character's mother was the illegitimate love child of a roving gypsy who was later framed for murder and hung—unless it affects the production.

Here is a good example of how mythology can be used. A 1940s Hollywood Gossip Columnist character from my Streetmosphere show often referred to her ownership of a button factory. She was always proud of the fact that in a time of unions, she used only nonunion child labor. She'd say that the little dears just loved to work twelve hours a day, and that the two cents a week really made a difference in their meager lives. The button factory was often referred to by other characters, and very nicely set up her foibles of *blindness and insensitivity*.

## Town Meetings

PURPOSE: To help focus social structure within the cast, and develop show mythology.

DESCRIPTION: The full cast of characters attend a "town meeting." Certain characters are chosen to perform the duties of speaker, moderator, and sergeant at arms. The speaker presents the problem the meeting has been called to discuss, and proposes a solution. Characters choose for themselves whether they are for or against the proposal and the discussion begins. The moderator's task is to make each point of view clear, and define common ground for a solution. The speaker's task is to defend the proposal. The sergeant at arm's task is to make sure that no one speaks out of turn. The scene ends when the meeting is adjourned, for whatever reason.

NOTES:  1. Coach actors to make *assumptions*, rather than *arguments*. They must *broaden the background of the issue* to support their position.
2. As information unfolds, each character assesses its

effect upon him- or herself and may change his or her opinion accordingly.

3. The social "station" must be respected throughout the exercise, although the dominance may shift as new information is revealed.

COMMENTS: Caution actors strongly against using their own values, opinion, or egos in the debate. Only those of their characters are to be used. Maintain the focus on creative assumptions rather than winning the argument. This exercise can get crazy sometimes, but the true nature of the characters will often come forth.

### Character Letters—Variation II

PURPOSE: To develop mythology.

DESCRIPTION: As in Character Letters—Variation I (see page 47), each actor in the group writes a one-page "letter," of any narrative form. It must be the character speaking, and a certain number of period vocabulary words, historical references, and period values must be incorporated. Actors must also incorporate other characters from the production, and use their relationships with them to motivate new background information. Letters are then read aloud.

NOTES: Conflicting information should not be a concern. Let the most interesting and playable information rise to the top. Then *set it in mud*, not stone.

COMMENTS: In addition to helping the history and language element, a great deal of group mythology can be created through the writing of these letters. It is most effective to continue this exercise on a daily basis for a while.

## *Building Encounters*

Everything you know about good improv scene work applies to the creation and performance of encounters. Encounters form the core of the interactive experience. This is where actors create together, often with no prior definition of action, guest-inclusive episodes of life within the subject. They are the primary reason ensemble is so necessary to the process. (See Chapter Fifteen of *The Art of Play*.)

New encounters are best derived from performance. In playing their character action with guests and exploring relationships with fellow characters, actors will be presented with ample, unsought possibilities. The process is then one of repeating and refining the raw material, during subsequent rehearsal or performance. Writing and rehearsal cannot surpass these spontaneous moments.

Nevertheless, encounter development must be undertaken during the rehearsal process. It is not as though good encounters cannot be created in rehearsal: they can. Undoubtedly, some will fly and some will fall; the results are often surprising. The important thing is to put an arsenal at the actors' disposal for the opening—to prime the pump, as it were.

FOCUSING THE ENCOUNTER

Often a successful bit of business is discovered, but the actors involved can't figure out where it goes or how it ends. This can happen for both an encounter devised in rehearsal or one come upon in performance. In either case, the routine may be presented in rehearsal to be workshopped into a finished encounter.

Plots in encounters are simple. They all seek need fulfillment and therefore boil down to the condition of "You have, I want." The *wanting* party is the character in need, the *having* parties are the other character(s) or the guest(s). *Focusing* an encounter merely means clarifying this point: who *has* and who *wants*? Each actor is likely to express, and pursue, his or her character's need in the scene, yet only one is central to the action.

For example, in a brush-up rehearsal for my 1940s Hollywood Streetmosphere show, three actresses came to me with a routine they had been playing with on the street. It involved the two Girls off the Bus trapped into reading a fan letter to a famous Starlet that was actually written for a male star. The actors knew the material would play well, but couldn't make the scene clear or find a suitable ending.

To focus their encounter, I began by *clarifying for them how each of their passions were at stake, what needs they were seeking to fulfill, and how foible or virtues were employed*.

In the encounter, the Starlet enters distraught over receiving a bad review for her latest film. Her passion is to be the most

adored star in Hollywood. Her need in this scene is to be complimented. Her foibles are vanity and manipulation. She meets up
with two Girls off the Bus; both their passions are to be discovered. It was decided that each has a need to ingratiate herself
with this famous star for possible advancement toward discovery.
In the scene, one uses her virtue of compassion, the other
employs her foible of naïveté.

As the scene begins, the Girls are finishing up a fan letter to
their favorite star, Clark Gable. The Starlet enters dramatically,
bemoaning the unfairness of the review. She begins fishing for
compliments from the two starstruck hopefuls and surrounding
guests. She makes her need and foibles clear. The Girls make
clear their need to ingratiate themselves with her, and endow a
guest as another hopeful. One Girl, prompted by her virtue of
compassion, falsely announces that the letter they are about to
send is to the Starlet's own fan club. At the Starlet's utmost insis-
tence, the three hopefuls read the fan letter intended for Gable. In
the process, the other Girl's naïveté results in the Starlet's vanity
being tortured. As they and the guest fake their way through the
letter, the naive Girl describes the Starlet as having a "manly
voice," "beautiful bushy eyebrows," and "adorably big ears."

At this point the actors didn't know where to go. Initially, the
action of the scene was muddy. After each character's needs
were identified, the action was much clearer, but they still didn't
know how to close the scene. The reason was that they had not
yet found the *premise* of the scene. Each actor was playing for her
own needs, which was fine, but they had no objective beyond
that. The question to be answered was, "Who is the scene about?"
Was it a story about one or the other Girl's chance at stardom, or
was it about a vain Starlet's comeuppance for her vanity and
manipulation?

Whose passion was at stake? All of them actually: each character's passion is always at stake. But whose passion was *central
to the action*? Most of the action seemed to revolve around the
Starlet's bad review and the gratification of her vanity. In fact, the
comic action of the letter being read would not play if the Starlet's
passion were not at stake. It is her need for compliments that
makes the device work. Once we focused the encounter by making the Starlet's fishing for compliments the premise, the ending
came immediately.

We reran the scene with this premise in mind; the action now
became crystal clear. When they came to the point where they
were stuck, the Starlet broke down, and in tears of rage vowed to

see that the Girls never worked in Hollywood. After she stormed out, the two Girls turned to the guest Girl and suggested she send their fan letter off to her "Uncle Clark." Ba da boom!

Could the premise have centered on one of the Girls off the Bus instead of the Starlet? Yes, it *could* have, but this focus would have entirely shifted the action and the ending of the scene accordingly. We would have ended up with a new encounter altogether.

*Foibles and Virtues in an Encounter* ■ In *character action*, passion attainment is foiled by the foible and aided or redeemed by the character's virtue, all within the neat package of a single character's relationship with the guest(s). In the multiple-character scene work of an encounter, it becomes more complex. Here foibles and virtues still affect the attainment of passion, but the only passion to be attained is now that of the character engaged in the premise: the character whose passion is most at stake. The foibles and virtues of *all* characters involved, in addition to input from the guest, interrelate to form the outcome. Which of the characters' virtues or foibles are employed, and how they are used, are simply a matter of what is right for the moment. Notice how in the example above, each character's foibles and virtues affected the premise in their own way.

*Identify the Plot Action* ■ There are only so many plots, so actors should not be too concerned with whether their plot idea is new and different. It is the execution that matters, the details that make it new: *how* did boy lose girl, *why* did boy lose girl, and *what* does that say to us?

Actors should seek to tell the emotional story, where the character struggles with relationships, needs, and desires. An emotional story uncovers more of the human heart and allows the audience to relate to the character on a personal level.

The character holds the keys to new and different action. Actors must be willing to follow their character, be open to its nature, and let it live. Some play merely for the situation, trying too hard to find new comic plots, and in the process throw away their belief in their characters. The richness and humanity of the character will always bring the actor to inspired new action. Work the character, not the plots; create, believe, and follow.

To help actors understand this, I take any number of encounters and reduce them to their essential plot action. The ultimate discovery is that there really aren't that many. The plot action of the encounter example above is *manipulation*. Hundreds may be devised with this same basic plot action, yet each encounter will have a unique quality and make a statement all its own. This is due to the *treatment* of the plot action, through the characters and their relationships.

Identifying the plot action can be a useful step in focusing an encounter. I have found that most plot action falls into these categories:

- Conquest
- Mischief
- Manipulation
- Seeking
- Obstacle to desire
- Instruction
- Misunderstanding
- Vengeance
- Competition

Emotional motives for plot action are generally as follows:

- Love
- Fear
- Jealousy
- Wrath
- Sloth
- Lust
- Greed
- Vanity
- Envy

These two lists encompass most of the plot action and their motives for almost any encounter. Although *they* can be boiled down to a simple list, the variety of human behavior in reaction to these circumstances cannot.

*Punch-list* ■ Here is a punch-list the director may use in focusing a new or existing encounter:

- How is each character's passion at stake?
- What are each character's needs in the scene?
- Whose passion is central to the action? (Who is the scene about?)
- What is the premise?

- What is the plot action?
- How are foibles and virtues used?
- What is the level of guest endowment and interaction?
- How can the guest be more active?
- Is the length appropriate?
- How good is the closure?

## Encounters from Attitudes

PURPOSE: To develop ideas for new encounters.

DESCRIPTION: This exercise proceeds just as the Character Attitudes Toward Characters (page 161) exercise does, except that once attitudes are established, actors use them as catalysts for new character interaction. While actors examine how attitudes on the list relate to one another's activities, new ideas will spring to life for possible conflicts between the characters. Actors then brainstorm activities or situations that will explore that conflict in an interesting or comic way, and how guests may be used in that activity. Using their occupational activities and character needs as a guide, new encounters can be created.

NOTES: Once a hot idea for an encounter is struck upon, actors brainstorm it from setup to closure and make notes on their ideas, then they get on their feet and run it.

COMMENTS: When one examines in a playful way the contrast between two characters' personality, occupation, and attitudes toward one another, ideas for encounters will practically suggest themselves.

### CLOSING ENCOUNTERS

Good closure is the goal of ending encounters. *Closure* ties up the loose ends and brings resolution to the conflict or a solution to the problem. It also carries the final statement. Polished encounters nearly always have a dependable close. But many encounters begin their lives as spontaneous moments in performance. Closing them can be one of the most difficult aspects of improvised encounters.

The experienced interactive actor develops a sense for when it is time to close an encounter. Experience teaches that good closure is valuable, and that it is always wise to take it when it comes. Learning to "hear the closure bell" and heed it can be vexing, because there are many temptations and fears to overcome.

Closure is missed when an actor doesn't pay attention to it. Closure is a deliberate act; it won't happen on its own. To miss a close, it only takes one actor in a scene not paying attention. Sometimes the ensemble gets overly selective about how to close. They struggle too long, and end up with what I call a *run-on encounter*. In a run-on encounter, the one-action-problem is prolonged or repeated past reason, to the point where something clearly should happen. Then the crowd begins to lose interest and will start to wander off. The ensemble must then cut their losses, before they completely bury the bit. If the ensemble cannot agree on the premise, a run-on encounter is likely to result. After all, how can they close an encounter when they don't agree on what they are closing?

Run-on encounters can happen even in the best of circumstances. When an encounter is going exceptionally well, actors may be reluctant to end it. There is nothing so gratifying as a large crowd enthralled with your routine. It can be hard to persuade actors to follow a reasonable close when they could easily continue to get laughs and applause. Interactive theatre places the curtain ropes squarely in the hands of the actor. The tried-and-true rule of "always leave them wanting more" doesn't always make sense while you are standing in the limelight.

This, however, does not alter the truism. The fact is that an audience will continue to give a positive response to a particularly interesting or comic scene *past* the point where they wonder when on earth it will end. As they walk away, they are likely to say to themselves, "That was fun but it didn't go anywhere." If the ensemble had provided a strong close at the height of the reaction, their audience would likely have left thinking, "That was great, and I loved the ending." One way leaves them eager to see more; the other leaves them thinking that they have seen enough.

Still, actors may argue, "Yeah, but we were on such a roll!" True, they should ride an exceptional moment for all it's worth, but there comes a point of diminishing returns. My suggestion is to end the routine before the audience looks for the end, let the crowd disperse for a moment or two, then try to reengage the same successful activity. Those guests who are truly willing to stay to see more will do so. The rest will move on more satisfied than if they had stayed. New audiences will step up, and more people will be entertained in the long run. In general, shorter successful encounters are better than longer successful ones.

Sometimes encounters run on because of a reluctance to exit. Actors can be reluctant to leave a partner alone at the end, even though a good closing line has been struck. They may feel they have run out and left the last one holding the bag, so to speak. They know that being the last character left in the midst of an expectant crowd can be daunting.

Often they misunderstand that they can just exit at that point. In interactive theatre, there are no curtains, blackouts, or wings to walk through. Most exits are just walking away from the crowd; there is nowhere else to go. Yet actors will be tricked into believing that because an audience is staring at them, they need to do something. I have often seen encounters brilliantly closed, then the lone actor left in the space suddenly continues the scene, and it flounders. It reminds me of a water-skier who falls and forgets to let go of the rope. If the scene is over, toss the audience an exit line and *leave!* This is the best way of getting a nice round of applause at the end.

*Common Closes* ■ Over the years I have noted certain standard closures. Outlining them may encourage actors to accept them.

- *Comeuppance:* This most popular one involves *just deserts* given to one character for their foibles. It requires only a "drat" and an exit.
- *Emo Endings:* This is closure that leads to an emotional catharsis. The character with the catharsis needs to exit with that emotion; any others quickly disperse.
- *Ironic Twist:* This usually involves a sudden disclosure that ties up the loose ends. Exits may incorporate the next actions each character intends to take.
- *The Chase:* This kind of closure leads to anger toward another character or a desperately needed activity offstage. Exit equals chase. Be sure the chase continues past the view of the audience.
- *Holding the Bag:* One character is left with the result of the conflict. The key to this exit is not to stand there any longer than it takes to deliver your exit line. If you do, you will be beginning a new scene.
- *Second Support Ending:* New information supplied by an entering character changes the nature of the situation or resolves it (a "deus ex machina"). As in the Ironic Twist, follow your new actions offstage.

## Three-Minute Scenes

PURPOSE: To train actors to condense their action and find closure.

DESCRIPTION: A location from the performance environment is chosen. Two-character scenes are presented that must find closure within three minutes. Scenes are timed, and a bell or clap is sounded for each minute that passes and a thirty-second warning before the three minutes are up. Characters must meet, find a premise, follow the rising action and conflict, and find resolution.

NOTES:  1. Scenes may be performed with two characters alone, or bystanders may be provided to be used as guests for interaction.
2. Actors may change the location of the scene, but may not create any space that is not actually present in the performance space of the production.

COMMENTS: Three minutes is longer than it sounds for a complete scene. Actors are likely to be surprised at just how much time they have. Nonetheless, this exercise will teach actors to find the action, cut to the chase, and close before the audience's attention wavers. This skill is crucial to successful interactive work!

# *Opening*

### BEFORE

The ensemble's frame of mind is crucial to the success of the first performance. Before opening, the ensemble needs positive encouragement. Try not to let last-minute production issues overshadow the spirit of temenos. Remind the cast before their first performance that there is nothing else they need to do, and nowhere else they need to be. Free them from worry, and let them know that their only concerns are those of trust, play, and joy.

## Jettison Baggage

PURPOSE: To clear the mind of anxiety before performance.

DESCRIPTION: The full group stands in a circle and joins hands. They close their eyes and breathe in deep continuous breaths, in through the nose and out through the mouth. The instructor asks them to take stock of their feelings and to identify any fears, anxieties, worries, self-judgment, anger, or any other negative emotion. They are instructed to remain relaxed and detached from these feelings, remaining only an observer. They are then asked to give each of these negative feelings a visual form. It may be an image, a symbol, or an object that represents to them each negative feeling or problem. They are to picture clearly in their mind each of these images. They then visualize a ball of intense white light centered in their chest or heart area, where these feelings are stored. From this light, a single beam of the same light extends to the center of the circle. Here a beam from each member of the circle converges and forms a larger ball of white light floating chest high in the center of the circle. One by one, they visualize sending the images of their negative emotion out along the beam of light and into the center hub. Now all the images of the entire circle exist in the center ball of light, not in themselves. The group then visualizes this ball of light slowly rising into the air, directed by the beams of light still emanating from their chests. The ball is raised high into the sky. They then prepare the most powerful *death ray* they can imagine, which when fired will obliterate the ball of light and all of the negative images it contains. When the ball of light is destroyed, it will sever the beam of light and separate the individuals from their negative feelings. On the count of three, the death ray is shot from each player's mind through a point in the forehead, between and above the eyes. The ball is destroyed in a cataclysmic explosion that annihilates all of their fears, worries, and anxieties. They then imagine a light from a quiet heart extending through their hands and encompassing the entire circle. The instructor affirms to the group that there is nowhere else they need to be, and nothing else they need to do but the performance at hand.

Another version of this exercise proceeds to the point where images of fears and worries are created, but in this exercise the fears are placed in a very strong lockable box. The players visually place the images within the box, lock it tightly, retain the key, and mentally set the box aside in a safe place for after the performance. In this way, worries and concerns are safely set aside, but they will be there where the actor left them, should they need to return to them later for resolution.

AFTER

After the opening, perhaps at the first postopening rehearsal, hear the ensemble's reaction to the performance. Let them relate their experiences. Prompt them to tell of their best experiences, then of their worst. Of their best work, clarify for them why it worked. Use these experiences as an opportunity to confirm ideas you presented in rehearsal. Encourage them to continue to capitalize on their successes.

Of the failures, remind them that their failures seem much larger to them than they did to the guests. Point out that guests do not possess the same context in which to compare their performance as they do. They tend to see the good as great, and the not-so-good as mildly interesting. Remind them that interactive theatre is by nature a series of hits and misses. Self-judgment for their misses will do far more damage to their performance in the long run than the misses themselves. Get them to focus on success, play, and joy.

Suggest that they enjoy their misses as well, since every miss provides a lesson with which they may improve their performance. Explore why each occurred, and focus on how these situations may be better approached next time. Encourage them to try valid ideas again with a new approach, even if they didn't work the first time.

Congratulations! You are now up and running. You have achieved a theatre that is truly alive and reactive to its audience. Your only task now, and it is an integral one, is to maintain it.

# Part II

# Show Maintenance

T he success of the interactive production is often only as good as the technique of the actors, the process. For this reason, ongoing rehearsals and workshops are even more important than they are in the conventional theatre. This section describes the kind of maintenance an interactive show needs after opening.

There are three basic areas. Maintaining the ensemble is crucial to the creation of temenos. Technique rehearsal involves brushing up on improv and interactive techniques; rehearsals are also necessary to support the continuing development of character and character relationships. Performance elements rehearsal is needed for endowments and lazzi, and encounter rehearsals support both the creation of new encounters and the perfection and maintenance of established encounters.

Rehearsals and workshops may take place in the rehearsal hall, but whenever possible they should be held on the actual set. This way encounters can be staged more precisely when needed, and workshops to reconnect characters to the environment or build mythology will be more effective.

# Maintaining the Ensemble 8

*It* cannot be overemphasized that trust holds the ensemble together and cannot long stand unattended. Like freedom, the price of creative harmony is vigilance.

## Group Trust

Establishing trust and mutual support within an ensemble is only the beginning. It must then be maintained. Volumes could be written on how to maintain trust within a group. I do not pretend to have all the answers, but I have learned a few things from experience that may be useful to you.

Whenever artists work collaboratively to achieve excellence, criticism will become part of the equation. Whether or not the director insists that criticism be handled only through him/her, ensemble members *will* talk. There is nothing intrinsically wrong with criticism; it can be a very constructive force. But it has its destructive aspects for which one must be watchful.

First, there is a difference between criticism and judgment. *Judgment* is the great destroyer of creativity, and when it comes in the guise of "constructive criticism" it can be most deadly. One actor must never judge another ensemble member's work, period. It is not for any actor to judge a fellow actor; in fact, it is not for anyone to judge anything within the temenos. Judgment statements start with the words "You should . . ." or "You don't. . . ." They imply that the speaker knows better and can usurp the collaborative spirit. It does this regardless of the intent of the speaker.

*Criticism*, as I define it for this discussion, is a statement of fact or an observation offered up to creative collaboration for improvement or enhancement. Criticism statements begin with "I think . . ." or "I feel. . . ." (Note: this does *not* include the statements "I think you should . . ." or "I feel you don't. . . .") Even better is criticism offered as interrogatives, such as "Could we look at. . . ?" or "Can we try. . . ?" In other words, they are applied to the *situation*, not the person. To change a judgment statement to a constructive criticism, merely remove the "you" and replace it with "I" or "we." Why? Responsibility in an ensemble is *shared*—all of it, all of the time.

An actor must not make a habit of admonishing him- or herself in front of the ensemble. There is nothing noble about self-blame; it makes the rest of the ensemble feel as if they are being begged to differ, or asked for compliments. Denial is no good either. Actors may speak of how "bad" their performance was if they do so with playfulness and forgiveness, and then only if it is true.

An actor should always apologize to other ensemble members for errors that may have affected them in performance. Be courteous enough to ask backstage if you stepped on any toes, and be ready to take yes for an answer and apologize. There is nothing wrong with being wrong, but it *is* wrong to always need to be right.

If there is anything I have learned from my long-run shows, the longest being seven days per week for seven years, it is that there is altogether too much talk and too little action. The constant need to discuss each and every issue becomes a black hole that sucks up the positive energy of the ensemble. I have seen this addiction to discussion turn good ensembles into an emotional morass, unnavigable by any creative intent.

Speak with actions not words! Make the attempt. Don't talk about it, do it. Say "I'm sorry" with *actions*. Say "I respect you" with *actions*. Say "I'll fix it" with *actions*. Say "I listen" by *listening*. Say "I'll do it" by *doing it*. Actions do speak louder than words. Words lose their value, but actions never do.

Once you speak with actions, you can communicate with deeds. Don't stop at making the attempt; accomplishments speak even louder than actions.

Ensembles can fall into the good/not good trap. Sure, anything with a destructive intent is "bad," but when qualifying your work, seeing the glass as half-full rather than half-empty does not negate or ignore the intent to fill it. There is no such thing as "not good." Everything has its own unique quality of "goodness," and everything can be better.

Some of the exercises in the "Trust" section of "Freeing the Imagination" (see pages 22–32) can be helpful in maintaining a positive bond between ensemble members. The "Hug, Rubs, and Compliments" exercise (see page 15) with the addition of what you like or admire about each other's work is a favorite of mine, as is the "Admiration Letters" exercise that follows.

A great part of the maintenance director's job is preserving the sacredness of the ensemble. Their role is to protect the temenos, often at the expense of their inclusion in it. Their duty is to protect play from the outside world. Whether it be budget problems, production changes, or unfair directives from above, it is this person's task to keep the ensemble free of all concerns not under its control, to conduct him- or herself with integrity, honesty, openness, and fairness, but at the same time to preserve innocence and play from the "real world." The creative process is an organism with a very thin and vulnerable membrane, and the director is often the sole protector of this scant fortification. The extent to which the director succeeds in defending this boundary is the extent to which the ensemble succeeds. It's a dirty job, but somebody has to do it. Make your refrain, "Relax, trust, and play!"

I post the following affirmations. Notice that each one begins with "I."

- I will put forth more energy onstage than off.
- I will establish the "givens," and be identifiable.
- I will make positive choices.
- I will take risks.
- I will fully commit to action, character, and period.
- I will accept everything offered me in performance.
- I will listen.
- I will initiate trust, without fear.
- I will work to include and celebrate the guests.
- I will let the guest answer my questions.
- I will be funny.
- I will fascinate.
- I will be available and approachable to all.

- I will compliment and praise my fellow actor.
- I will always endeavor to make the other person look good.
- I will be open to the spirit of camaraderie, play, and fun.
- I will celebrate in performance.
- I will exercise good communication.
- I will be supportive, respectful, and kind to my fellow actor backstage.
- I will be flexible in my thinking.
- I will find solutions to problems instead of complaining.
- I will not judge others or myself.
- I will remember to maintain my perspective.
- I will work to the top of my intelligence.
- I will act in a professional manner.

### Admiration Letters

PURPOSE: To build or rebuild mutual admiration, communication, and ensemble trust.

DESCRIPTION: Each actor is asked to write a few sentences on what they honestly admire most about each of their fellow ensemble members. They are to include what they admire both about their work and about them personally. When the letters are completed, they are copied and distributed among the cast. (Each actor's admiration letter includes a paragraph on each other ensemble member, and is copied and distributed to every player in its entirety.) These letters should not be read aloud, but time in rehearsal should be set aside for actors to read them.

COMMENTS: This exercise can be an incredibly powerful rebuilder of ensemble by reaffirming the positive aspects of the actors' relationships. As time goes on, it seems that only the negative aspects of the work or the relationship surface. Time taken to reaffirm what is good about those relationships places the negative back in perspective, and reopens blocked energy.

## Adding New Ensemble Members

Little is preserved of how the improvisers of the commedia dell'arte in the fourteenth and fifteenth centuries plied their craft. But in what remains, there is a discussion of the difficulties of adding a new company member to an existing ensemble, many of whom have worked together for a long time. The problems they had then are the same ones you'll encounter today. It takes some time for the new improviser to fit in with the energies of the ensemble. It takes patience and a good deal of support and forgiveness on the ensemble's part, for the path is not always a smooth one, despite everyone's best intentions.

What makes this even more difficult for the existing ensemble members is that once the new member has attuned him- or herself to the rhythms of the ensemble, those rhythms have been permanently altered. Each time a new member is added, it becomes a different ensemble. Previous ensemble members must be willing not only to accept the new input, but also to let go of some of the patterns that they have played before. My experience has been that the time it takes for a new member to become acclimated to the group often runs longer than the patience of the ensemble. Despite members' understanding and good intentions, an ensemble will usually tire of the inconvenience that this fitting-in process causes them. The director must be aware of this and be prepared to be supportive of both new and old members.

Most ensembles welcome new members with open arms, because it means new blood and fresh ideas for them to play with. Other less supportive ensembles may exact a toll from the new member by putting them through a period of "hazing," during which the new person is supposed to somehow prove his or her worth to the group before they will be accepted. These are not the rules of temenos. Temenos invites a new player in with joy and welcoming. The trust is given, not earned. Judgment is never imposed. Only in this way can new members be free enough to explore their own creativity deeply enough to be of service to the group.

Make every attempt to prevent the ensemble from segregating the new member verbally by calling them the "new person." Whenever possible, I insist on calling them by name and avoid any mention of them as new people. I try my best to treat them as though they have always been trusted members of the ensemble. This is usually enough for them to believe that they are, and for others to accept them as such. Otherwise, the label of "new kid" will stick with an ensemble member until the next "new kid" comes along, even if it takes months.

A director can do some things to make the transition easier for new ensemble members. Make them understand that they need to make strong assumptions in performance. It is more important that their assumptions be made with confidence and conviction than that they be successful. The ensemble will find it much easier to forgive mistakes than timidity or dependence.

Ask new ensemble members to think in terms of *leading* a scene, rather than following. Their tendency will be to be careful not to step on toes, but this will only be seen as tentativeness. Let them know that they are as in charge as any other ensemble member, that they are as free to lead a scene.

If I have several new cast members to work into an ensemble, I will sometimes impose a brief moratorium on all but the newest routines. This puts the whole company, old and new members, on an even footing. For a day or a week, they can only do the encounters that the new members learned in rehearsal.

Working new cast members into old routines has its problems as well. Actors can be more set in their ways with the older, more polished encounters. To their credit, they have a keener sense of which choices play better, and this must not be ignored. However, a new actor will always work a little differently and has the right to explore his or her part. The correct position of the director is to have a healthy respect for what works and a strong openness to new input.

Whenever possible, add new members in groups rather than one at a time. It will greatly decrease the workload in getting the ensemble back on track. Make it a point in rehearsals to review all of the character choices of the company. This way new ensemble members get a clear picture of the characters they will be dealing with. Use this time also as a chance for the entire ensemble to discuss and update character choices and relationships. Ask old ensemble members to bring out the character notes they made when they developed their characters, and note the ways in which their characters have grown. They may be surprised at just how different their ensemble is from when it was first rehearsed. This is a good way of giving everyone a sense of rebirth as new members enter.

## Backstage Behavior

Nothing throughout the run affects the performance more than the ensemble's treatment of each other backstage. To me, the rules of behavior backstage are every bit as important as the rules of behavior onstage. This is never more true than with improvised theatre. It is impossible to engage in creative play in front of an audience with the same person who abused, belittled, ignored, or resented you backstage. Regardless of your professionalism, there are emotional blocks at work here that are insurmountable.

One union show I was directing was approaching contract renewal time during a phase of bad backstage behavior. I went to the Actors' Equity Association, and they ruled, informally, that negative behavior backstage directly affects the quality of an improvised performance, and is therefore grounds for dismissal or nonrenewal. Once I made the cast aware of this, they took their backstage behavior more seriously. They seemed to feel they had a right to treat each other poorly backstage, because they treated each other well onstage.

A temenos must exist whenever the group is together, whether they are onstage or off. The mechanisms of creative play cannot be engaged until this happens. In my productions, actors are obviously free to do and say whatever they please outside the theatre, but once they arrive for performance, they may only use what I call "positive speech."

Complaints are not allowed unless they come with suggestions for improvement. Views or observations may not be phrased negatively, e.g., "This dressing room is always a mess," but positively, as in, "This dressing room really needs cleaning." Negative speech on *any* topic is frowned upon even if it has nothing to do with the production.

These rules are imposed solely for creative purposes. It has been proven that a positive mental attitude promotes better creative flow than a negative one. It has also been proven that the type of language spoken or heard affects our mental attitude significantly.

# *Maintaining the* 9
# *Technique*

O ngoing workshops should be provided to keep the ensemble's skill sharp. These should include both improvisation and interactive technique.

## *Skills Rehearsals*

### IMPROVISATION

Merely because an improviser achieves a certain skill level does not mean that he or she will always use it. Veteran improvisers are as capable of bad technique as novices are, but they do so for different reasons. A novice's technique may falter for lack of knowledge or experience, and a veteran's technique may falter because of complacency, overconfidence, or even boredom.

Make your workshops as fun and challenging as you can, but don't allow the veteran performer to dissuade you from covering the basics.

### INTERACTIVE TECHNIQUE

Maintaining interactive technique should also be reviewed and workshopped on a regular basis. As ensemble members build a very close rapport over time, a director may see guest interaction in encounters dwindle. If one actor's style and timing are well known, another may unconsciously capitalize on that strength to the exclusion of the guest. Actors need to be reminded to use these strengths to better include the guest.

It is admittedly problematic to workshop guest interaction in a postopening rehearsal hall. Still, there are many areas that an ingenious director can devise workshops for. These may include the following:

- Exploring outward, inclusive energy
- Recognizing proper and improper ways of making physical contact with a guest
- Reducing interpersonal barriers
- Listening to the guests and using their assumptions
- Endowing the guest
- Visualizing the guest in period

Interactive technique workshops can also help identify dead ends for actors. Here the director can help them with their own weaknesses and find specific solutions to recurring problems.

## Maintaining Character

Of constant concern is having the ensemble maintain character. There are so many distractions in an interactive performance environment, and the interactive actor plays so close to the self, that there is an ever-present pull that draws the actor out of character as time goes on.

### BREAKING CHARACTER BY COMMENTING ON THE PERFORMANCE

One deadly sin is commenting on the performance *in performance*. Actors sometimes don't consider this breaking character since the character itself makes the comments, but the reference breaks the reality of the show. For instance, one character makes a mistake of some kind, and a partner responds, "I never got it in rehearsal either."

The standard defense of this kind of comment is that it got a laugh; indeed, it often does. One definition of comedy describes it as an odd juxtaposition of ideas, or a sudden change in points of view. Certainly comments like this one fit that description. The sudden shift from a theatrical reality to actors commenting on their work is intrinsically funny. This does not alter the fact that they have broken the illusion that the character exists to create.

## COMMITTING TO CHARACTER IN COMIC MOMENTS

In a similar vein, some actors will break up in performance. A performer giggling over something that goes wrong will always elicit laughter from the audience. But the question is, is it the kind of laughter an actor should seek? Harvey Korman made a career out of it on "The Carol Burnett Show." In fact, the other cast members made a point of cracking Harvey up whenever they could. It was great for laughs, and great for ratings, but a network variety show is a different animal than a live theatrical production. Like me, you may love "Harvey Kormanisms," but they should not be encouraged in an interactive production, or, like a merry cancer, they will slowly devour every cell of believability in the performance.

There is another angle to approach comedy. Rather than pander to the comic moment, *live it*. True character comedy is funny because the characters involved *believe* in the moment. Their surprise, or confusion, or frustration is sincere. Sincerity in the face of absurdity is *funny*. This is the comedy of Buster Keaton, Jackie Gleason, or Lily Tomlin. When Lucille Ball was asked what advice she would give to an aspiring comedian, she answered in three words: "Believe, believe, believe." Sincerity is the hallmark of character comedy. It is through this that the human element is exposed and humor comes to mean more than just laughter.

## THE SEPARATE PERFORMANCE OBJECTIVES OF PLAY AND COMEDY

The intent of an interactive character is to amuse. There are many ways to amuse, and the actor must not make the mistake of believing that the only time the character is valid is when that actor is getting laughs. I caution actors about this often, because the need for the actor to get laughs eclipses many of the more subtle character choices that can be made. I have often seen characters completely disappear for the sake of a laugh. It must be remembered that these characters do not exist for comedy's sake, but rather that comedy flows from them. Comedy serves the character, not the other way around.

## CHARACTER THINNING

*Character thinning* is when the characterization partially drops. The *seams* of the character show. It shows first in the eyes. Meeting a performer face to face is a visceral experience. When they look straight into your eyes and begin telling you about their latest extraordinary experience, all theatrical convention is stripped away. They have only their force of will to make you believe. If you can look back into their eyes and see an *actor* performing for you, the magic is lost, or it never really begins. If, instead, you see a fully developed and credible character staring back at you, it is a delightful shock *not* to see an actor. It is truly as if the character has come to life.

If I ask actors to describe the thrill of performing an intimate scene on stage, they will often describe their fascination at their partner suddenly taking on the life of the character and not seeming like the actor at all, and of feeling lost in the illusion. That is the same feeling guests get when they look into the actor's eyes and see only the character. In some ways we are giving the audience a chance to see what it is like on our side of the proscenium.

When you cannot see the seams of the character, you cannot see where the actor leaves off and the character begins. Suddenly the illusion is created for you and a temenos appears. You actually experience that character's personal adventure, in a way that is very compelling. At that moment, this person in front of you suddenly becomes a real outlaw from the nineteenth century; the world around you becomes the American West, and not just an interactive event you paid to visit. In that moment, it creates a total illusion where you can suspend your disbelief and allow everything created around you to be *real*.

## THE PERSONA CHARACTER

A real pet peeve of mine that I see from time to time in interactive shows is what I call the *persona character*. It usually happens in audience participatory types of street theatre, rather than in interactive characterizations, but it is common enough in any interactive work to be a pitfall of some concern. It happens when the characterization is *nonspecific*; it becomes no more than an exaggerated, outer personality of the actor himself. The actor does not don the cloak of another personality, but simply inflates his/her own presence. The actor may wear the costume, and speak the language; he or she may even be quite effective and engaging, but to the viewer it seems as if the actor is speaking through a thin veil of a characterization. It is more like watching a barker at a side show than the product of a theatrical illusion.

It is a destructive choice for most interactive situations because it prevents the audience from believing in the illusion. If the actor gives them the sense of "I am an actor, look at me, aren't I clever and interesting," the guest is then unable to step into the illusion of the show. A persona characterization pushes the audience away from the suspension of disbelief, rather than toward it. If it is worth stepping onstage to perform for an audience, it is worth presenting a true and believable character.

Persona characters are usually the product of laziness, or burnout from playing too long a character with too little challenge to it. It is absolutely true of interactive theatre that if the characterizations are not believable, then neither is the entire environment. It is just as jarring to the audience's sense of belief as it would be to go to a stage play and suddenly see the actors stop and converse with the stage manager about what their next lines are. An actor out of character is an actor out of character, no matter what the style.

The audience may be amused by persona characters, but these characters will never capture their imaginations. Persona characters don't play by the rules, and so spoil the temenos. And this is too bad, because if only the actors presented a real and credible character, they would find that the audience would be so much more enthralled by whatever they did.

### CHARACTER REHAB REHEARSALS

As mentioned earlier, an occasional character rehab session can be beneficial. In this rehearsal each character's individual choices are reviewed and updated. Character relationship exercises are repeated, and the most current relationships are established for the entire ensemble. Often relationship changes between two characters are not readily apparent to other ensemble members, so the rest of the ensemble may be slow to adapt to those characters' new ways of dealing with one another. This workshop helps clear up any confusion.

### CREATING CHARACTER OBJECTIVES

New objectives can be toyed with to keep characters on their toes. In one show I placed a permanent board in the green room for the actors to list specific objectives that they would play in performance. These objectives could include focusing on a particular aspect of technique; providing themselves with overriding motivation for a particular day or set; creating a new element of personal mythology or background to explore; providing an emotional objective, etc. I then required that these objectives change weekly so that each week of performance a veteran character had something completely new to deal with.

For interactive events I sometimes imposed a castwide objective for the day. These "dailies" would introduce a new problem or challenge that each character in the cast had to deal with, either individually or collectively. In my 1940s Hollywood show we had a box of dailies written on three-by-five cards. From time to time, we pulled them out and chose such things as "Tonight is Oscar Night," or "Sam Goldwyn's Birthday," or "A winning lottery ticket was lost on Hollywood Boulevard."

Dailies are not as useful in an interactive play because they may distract characters from the execution of the plot line. However, playing personal objectives can make characters quite memorable.

### WORKING THE CHARACTER'S EMOTIONAL LEVEL

Characters can tend to become emotionally flat over time. Working the emotional level of the character in workshops can help to bring back a lost vitality. It takes more physical energy to present a heightened emotion, and actors can simply become lazy. This lack of energy or heightened emotion has a noticeable effect on the audience's response to character interaction.

There is an energy exchange between performer and audience. One builds upon the other, but it is the actor who must prime the pump. I once listened to an ensemble complain about how dull and lifeless the guests were that day. I instructed them to forget about receiving energy from the guests, and focus instead on throwing as much energy as they could in the first five minutes of the set. They did so and were astonished at the guests' sudden enthusiasm, which continued to build throughout the set. Upon their return, I informed them that it was *they* who were dull and lifeless, not the guests.

## Character Relationships

### PROBLEM RELATIONSHIPS

Every so often two actors have a difficult time relating on set. The characters don't seem to have much in common, or else they always seem to have difficulty supporting one another in a scene. The problem may not be between the actors, but between the characters. The relationship that they established may not be a positive one, or it may simply not work well. Take the time in these cases to examine carefully what each actor's perception of the relationship is, and encourage them to acquire new aspects of the relationship, or redesign it entirely. Let them know that it is all right to change the relationship if it is not working. A new relationship can completely transform their work.

REVIEW OF STARTING POINTS

Another good brushup is reviewing the starting points of the character's relationships. This is where the character goes through key points that must be established in performance for the audience to understand their relationship. As time goes on, actors take their character relationships for granted and make the unconscious assumption that the audience understands them as well. A good exercise for this is having the characters play out the moments of their first meeting. They then play through the scene until each of the key starting points have been created.

## First Meeting Scenes

PURPOSE: To review information needed to establish character relationships in performance.

DESCRIPTION: All group members mill and seethe in character, throughout the rehearsal space. They are to encounter fellow characters one at a time and initiate a scene where the characters are meeting for the very first time. In each encounter, actors establish a location that is appropriate to their first meeting, wherever that may be. They then play out a scene that motivates each aspect of their predetermined relationship, revealing how they were formed. Once this is concluded, the actor encounters another character and an appropriate location is established, etc. The entire group can play out scenes simultaneously, continuing until all characters have met all other characters "for the first time." After this, the instructor may give characters time to pair up once again and discuss specific ways they can reveal their character's relationship in performance.

NOTES:  1. In this exercise realities overlap. Each pair of characters create their surroundings in whatever way best
suits their scene.
2. Actors are not setting in stone how their characters
originally met, but are playing out only one possible
past history.

COMMENTS: Motivating character relationships in this way
gives actors a better connection to their partners by creating a
shared memory. It is as valuable for older ensembles wishing to
renew their relationships as it is for a new ensemble first establishing them. It may also create some interesting elements of
mythology.

SHOPPING

One of the weakest choices a character can make is to simply sidle
up to another character(s) engaged in lazzi or encounters and see
what happens. If they are to enter the scene, they should use good
second support. Otherwise, the mere presence of the character
will draw focus and confuse the scene. Characters should either *be
there* or *not be there*, and always in a very definite way.

The worse kind of these "shoppers" gain entry to an
encounter by absorbing the action present. They seem to just
appear and take part in the action without invitation, or any motivation for being there.

Another form of shopper silently tags along and waits to be
addressed or included. This places the responsibility on another
character to draw them in and motivate their presence. This kind
of passive behavior can be annoying to other ensemble members.

A third kind of shopper stands to the side and merely asks
questions. These shoppers believe they are taking part in the
scene, but by not making new assumptions, they are only requiring the other characters in the scene to work harder.

If the shopping habit is not addressed quickly, the actor
stands a chance of being avoided by other ensemble members,
who will feel resentful and overworked. Once this happens, the
situation will only compound itself. In order to be included, shoppers will have to resort to shopping all the more, pushing them
farther away from the ensemble.

## *Maintaining Style*

Style workshops are also an important part of ongoing rehearsals. They may be conducted as often as the director feels necessary, but they should be touched on from time to time. The precision of the actors' period movement, dialect, and language use can fade if not reviewed. It is particularly important to continue work on the lexicon or vocabulary of the period language and the history of the period. These two items can never be workshopped enough. They not only add dimension to the performance, but also provide ideas for new action and turns of phrase.

# *Maintaining the* *10*
# *Performance*
# *Elements*

O ngoing rehearsals should address each performance element—character action, endowments, lazzi, encounters, scenarios, and attractions—within the context of illuminating the subject and themes of the production.

As the production evolves, the best moments must be captured and honed; the worst moments must be identified and eliminated. This procedure must be performed continually.

Scenario and attractions should be maintained in whatever way best suits the production. Technique rehearsals will cover most aspects of maintaining character action. Be sure to review character passion and needs every now and then, however. Believe it or not, actors can become so centered on routines that they forget their needs and ignore their passion. When this happens, their playing becomes dictated by the routines themselves and can make their characterization wander or become shallow.

Not only should the cast maintain a good stock of endowment characters, they must use them. Without constant care, this too can wane. The extent to which they use endowments is the extent to which your show is interactive. Be watchful. Try making a game of it; ask the cast to keep track of how many times a guest they endowed actually filled their character's need. Be creative.

In some interactive events where the show was done in sets, I would from time to time forbid actors to do anything other than throw endowments for one whole set. They could not talk to any other character unless directed to by a guest after receiving an endowment.

Again, a good stock of lazzi should be maintained in the actor's log. Make sure actors are maintaining those logs regularly or else many a good lazzo will be lost. Lazzi tend to have lives of their own, but they can be workshopped to make them clearer. New lazzi can be developed through examining active choices and playing them in scenes with other characters.

## Encounters

Encounters are the meat and potatoes of the production. The scenario guides the story of the interactive play, but even here the encounter is what brings the action of the story to the guest. In interactive events, encounters alone make up the collective story of life in the environment. The collection of encounters each guest sees creates their theatrical experience, so make sure that they reveal the subject and its themes, and that they are numerous and of good quality.

Most of the ongoing rehearsals will be taken up with focusing encounters as discussed earlier, or with devising new ones to try out in the next performance.

### ESTABLISHING AND REESTABLISHING

I have found that as the production run goes on, actors need constant reminding that what they know about their character, its relationships, and the encounters they perform does not magically leap into the minds of the audience. Establishing the basic information of the character's occupation (who) and the action at hand in the encounter (what) must be done at the beginning and throughout the encounter, no matter how many times they perform it.

Drilling the ensemble on establishing and reestablishing character and action in their encounters is a regular feature in my rehearsals. The following exercise works well.

## Face Value Reestablishing Scene

PURPOSE: To develop the skill of reestablishing key information in an encounter.

DESCRIPTION: A location for the scene is chosen. An actual location within the performance environment is best. Players One and Two enter the space and begin a scene in character. They follow their needs and the needs of their partner, until a premise for the scene is found. As they develop the action, they are to pursue two overriding objectives for their scene. First, they are to establish as clearly, specifically, and early as they can, their names, occupations, the location (time and space) of the scene, and the action at hand. Second, as the scene continues, they are to *reestablish* that information as often as they can, without stopping the actual flow of action.

NOTES: 1. Actors must endeavor to reestablish information as often as possible, but in a slightly different way each time, without sounding like a broken record.
2. Any viewer seeing less than a minute from any portion of the scene ought to be able to relate this basic information.

COMMENTS: There are few skills more important in interactive performance than that of reestablishing information in an interesting and nonrepetitive manner.

### CATALOGUING, ARCHIVING, AND ROTATING ENCOUNTERS

Along with the other logs, keep a catalogue of all polished encounters. If you maintain no other log, maintain this one. It may seem to the cast that regularly played encounters are impossible to forget, but the fact is they are not always played with regularity. As the run of the production continues, some encounters fall out of favor, become stale, or are indeed forgotten. Only by maintaining an up-to-date listing and description of encounters can the ensemble be assured of not losing one of its little gems.

An encounters log (see page 200) can be invaluable to new members being worked into the production. Certainly they will want to develop new encounters with the ensemble, but they will need a starting point. Many encounters become standard, and a listing can help a new member in getting up to speed quickly.

During long runs, actors may become bored with encounters that are otherwise very effective. The best course of action is to set those encounters aside and give them a rest, while the ensemble challenges itself to come up with new ones. When these archived encounters are brought back later they will usually regain their lost vitality. Sometimes great new improvements are made, leaving the cast to wonder why they ever set them aside in the first place.

Ensembles can also get themselves into ruts by repeating only their favorite encounters. The director may elect to arbitrarily rotate encounters to be certain that all of them are getting good play. I recommend that if a rotation is used, there still be ample room for the ensemble's favorites. There is a distinct advantage to allowing a cast to exercise their own choice in playing what gives them the most joy. A good balance of challenge and choice is best.

Use these logs for keeping an up-to-date record of all polished encounters.

## Encounters Log

Catalogue *all* encounters for the production. Use to archive and rotate encounters. Provide enough description so that they may be reconstructed by new cast members.

**Title:**_____

**Description:** _____

_____

_____

_____

_____


**Title:**_____

**Description:** _____

_____

_____

_____

_____

## Encounters Log For Characters

Catalogue *all* encounters your character is involved in. Provide enough description so that you are sure to remember the encounter and your role in it.

**Title:** _____

**Description:** _____

_____

_____

_____

_____

_____

**Title:** _____

**Description:** _____

_____

_____

_____

_____

_____

**Title:** _____

**Description:** _____

_____

_____

_____

_____

**Title:** _____

**Description:** _____

_____

_____

_____

_____

# A Final Note

*T*he doors you will open with this technique will uncover a greater mystery than the technique itself can explain. In essence, it creates a safe and sacred place for the artist to work, free of fears, judgment, and doubt—a temenos. Opening a channel to one's creative power engages a positive and life-changing force. Interactive theatre notwithstanding, work inside the temenos actualizes a truer self for the artist. Endeavors of this kind are worthy of respect, even reverence. They are mysteries no book can fully encompass.

The more I explore and use this technique, the more I realize just how fragile we are. As director or teacher of this technique, use gentleness and patience; you will be rewarded for it. Consider carefully your motives and integrity before you help another to unlock these doors we so carefully bar. This path leads the artists back to their initial innocence, their connection to their creative source. It is a vulnerable place. The barricades you help to remove were placed there for a reason; they protect this sacred place. I caution you only to take your role as protector of the temenos seriously, and to acknowledge its responsibility.

# Exercise Index